P9-CBB-560

SAN FRANCISCO

JEFFREY KENNEDY

Left **San Francisco Museum of Modern Art** Right **Surfers, Pacific Ocean**

LONDON, NEW YORK,
MELBOURNE, MUNICH AND DELHI
www.dk.com

Produced by Sargasso Media Ltd, London

Reproduced by Colourscan, Singapore
Printed and bound by
South China Printing Co. Ltd., China

First published in Great Britain in 2003
by Dorling Kindersley Limited
80 Strand, London WC2R 0RL
A Penguin Company

**Reprinted with revisions
2004, 2006, 2007
Copyright 2003, 2007 ©
Dorling Kindersley Limited, London**

A CIP catalogue record is available
from the British Library.

ISBN 1-40531-736-1
ISBN 978-1-40531-736-8

Within each Top 10 list in this book, no
hierarchy of quality or popularity is implied.
All 10 are, in the editor's opinion, of
roughly equal merit.

Floors are referred to throughout in
accordance with American usage; ie. the
"first floor" is at ground level.

Contents

San Francisco's To **P** 10

JACKET: Front Cover: **ALAMY IMAGES**: Dennis Hallinan clb; naglestock.com: main image; **DK IMAGES**:
Andrew McKinney bl; Spine: **DK IMAGES**: Andrew McKinney; Back: **DK IMAGES**: Andrew McKinney tc;
Neil Lukas tl; Robert Vente tr.

Left **View from Nob Hill** Right **Enrico's restaurant, North Beach**

Left **Golden Gate Bridge** Right **Japanese Tea Garden, Golden Gate Park**

 Key to abbreviations
Adm *admission charge* **Free** *no admission charge* **Dis. access** *disabled access*

3

SAN FRANCISCO'S TOP 10

ᵀᴼᴾ10 San Francisco's Highlights

San Franciscans will, rather candidly, admit that they are the most fortunate people on earth, the occasional earthquake notwithstanding; and most visitors, after a few days of taking in the sights and sounds of this magnificent city, will agree. Ask anyone who has been here and they will tell you it's their favorite US city. The geographical setting evokes so much emotional drama, the light seems clearer, the colors more vivid, the cultural diversity of the ethnic neighborhoods so captivating and inviting, that it's a place almost everyone can fall in love with at first sight.

Golden Gate Bridge **1**

The much-loved symbol of the city and of California's place on the Pacific Rim, the Golden Gate Bridge is the third-largest single span bridge in the world, connecting San Francisco to Marin County *(see pp8–9)*.

2 Cable Cars

San Francisco's little troopers have endured technological progress, and are now the only system of the kind in the world that still plays a daily role in urban life *(see pp10–11)*.

3 Fisherman's Wharf

Despite rampant tourism and commercialization, the saltiness and authenticity are still to be found here if you take time to look. The views of the bay are unmatched, and you'll have an opportunity to sample some great seafood *(see pp12–13)*.

4 Alcatraz

Although it was a federal prison for just under 30 years, the myth of "The Rock" continues to capture the imagination of visitors. Even if exploring prison life holds no appeal, the ferry ride makes it well worth a visit *(see pp14–17)*.

Lincoln Park

Sutro Heights Park

GEARY BOULEVARD

GREAT HIGHWAY

Richmond

CALIFORN

GEARY BOU

FULTON STREET

Golden Gate Park **6**

LINCOLN WAY

Sunset District

SUNSET BLVD

19TH AVENUE

7TH AVENUE

miles ⌐ 0 ⌐ km

Pre

GOLDEN GATE BRIDGE FRWY

BOULEVARD

LINCOLN

PARK PRESIDIO BOULEVARD

25TH AVENUE

Chinatown
5 The exotic feel of one of the world's largest Chinese communities outside of Asia makes this a magnet for locals and visitors alike *(see pp18–19)*.

Golden Gate Park
6 The city boasts one of the largest public parks in the world, with natural beauty and fine museums *(see pp20–23)*.

Grace Cathedral
7 Dominating Nob Hill with its timeless beauty, San Francisco's favorite cathedral offers a host of awe-inspiring and historic treasures, including Italian Renaissance masterpieces and stained-glass windows *(see pp24–5)*.

San Francisco Museum of Modern Art
8 Second only to New York City's Museum of Modern Art, San Francisco's newest architectural landmark houses 20th-century masterworks of painting, sculpture, and photography, and the edgiest digital installations *(see pp26–9)*.

The Wine Country
10 So internationally recognized have the wines from this region become that French, Italian, and Spanish winemakers have all established vineyards here. A day trip or a longer stay shouldn't be missed *(see pp32–5)*.

Mission Dolores
9 The city's oldest building is also the only intact chapel among the 21 California missions that Father Junipero Serra founded in the late 18th century. Its founding just days before the Declaration of Independence makes San Francisco older than the US *(see pp30–31)*.

🔟 Golden Gate Bridge

As with most of the world's wonders, many said that the Golden Gate Bridge could never be built – the span was too wide, the ocean too powerful and deep, and the cost too great. But to many more, the Golden Gate, the name John Fremont gave the splendid strait in 1844 (see p39), demanded the realization of its dream bridge. In 1872, railroad tycoon Charles Crocker first conceived the idea, but it took a visionary engineer, Joseph Strauss, to put forth a realistic proposal in 1921. After 10 years of opposition from all quarters, funding was finally secured from A.P. Giannini, founder of the Bank of America (see p39). The bridge opened in 1937, and has been an emblem of San Francisco and America's icon on the Pacific ever since.

Marin Vista Point

🍴 For a uniquely powerful view of the bridge while enjoying a Sunday champagne brunch, opt for one of the many cruises on the Bay, departing from the Embarcadero Pier and Sausalito. Excellent purveyors are Signature Yacht Events (415-788-9100, www.signaturesf. com), and Seaward (415-331-3214, www.callofthesea. org).

- Map C1
- (415) 923-2000
- www.goldengate.org
- Cruises operate Mar–Oct

Top 10 Features

1. Deco Style
2. Maintenance
3. Fort Point Lookout
4. Marin Vista Point
5. Star Turns in Movies
6. Protective Barriers
7. Building the Bridge
8. Bridge Celebrations
9. Hiking and Biking
10. Toll System

1 Deco Style

The bridge owes its striking style to the consulting architects Irving F. Morrow and his wife Gertrude. They simplified the pedestrian railings to uniform posts placed far enough apart to allow an unobstructed view.

2 Maintenance

Repairing and painting the bridge *(above)* is an ongoing task. The paint protects it from the high salt content in the air, which corrodes the steel components.

3 Fort Point Lookout

On the city side stands an 1861 fort *(below)*. This spot provides a view of the soaring underside of the structure and the pounding waters of the ocean.

The orange color was actually the original rust-proof undercoat, but it complements the natural setting so well that it was kept.

4 Marin Vista Point
Crossing from the San Francisco side, pull off just before you reach the end of the bridge and take in the startling panorama from the specially constructed Vista Point and look back at the hills and spires of the city. If there's fog, note how the bridge's tower tops disappear in the mist.

6 Protective Barriers
The Golden Gate Bridge is the number one spot in the world for suicides. As yet there are no effective preventative barriers but there are bars *(above)* for general safety.

7 Building the Bridge
Joseph Strauss introduced the use of hard hats, goggles, and safety belts for the first time, as well as a vast safety net under the bridge, which saved 19 workers.

10 Toll System
Beginning May 28, 1937, the toll to cross the bridge was 50 cents each way, with a 5-cent charge if a car had more than three passengers. The toll is currently $2.50 per axle, only charged to city-bound traffic *(below)*.

5 Star Turns in Movies
The bridge has starred in many movies, most notably Alfred Hitchcock's *Vertigo*, in which James Stewart pulls Kim Novak from the raging surf, just east of Fort Point *(see p53)*. In the James Bond movie, *A View To A Kill*, Grace Jones and 007 battle it out, both of them clinging to the bridge's aerial heights.

8 Bridge Celebrations
The bridge opened on May 28, 1937, with some 200,000 pedestrians. Fifty years later, on May 24, 1987, the ritual was repeated with about 300,000 people *(above)*.

9 Hiking and Biking
No visit to San Francisco would be complete without a walk or bike-ride across at least part of the bridge.

The Statistics
The length of the steel wires used to make the cables of the bridge is enough to circle the earth three times. It is also brilliantly "over-engineered" and is said to be five times stronger than it needs to be to withstand the winds and tides it endures daily. At the time it was built, it was the longest suspension bridge in the world (it still ranks seventh) and took just over four years to build. More than 41 million vehicles cross the bridge annually, streaming across six lanes of traffic, along its 1.7-mile (2.7-km) length. The bridge is equipped with two foghorns, each with a different pitch, and 360-degree flashing red beacons. The bridge has been closed due to high winds only three times in its history.

 Pedestrians may access the east sidewalk 5am–9pm daily. In-line skaters and skateboards are not allowed.

🔟 Cable Cars

It's impossible not to love these sturdy little vestiges of another age, as they valiantly make their merry yet determined way up the city's precipitous hills. Yet these San Francisco icons came perilously close to being completely scrapped in 1947, when a "progressive" mayor announced it was time for buses to take their place. An outraged citizenry, under the leadership of "cable car vigilante" Mrs. Friedell Klussman, eventually prevailed, and the whole system was declared a National Historic Landmark in 1964. In the early 1980s, the tracks, cables, power plant, and cars all underwent a massive $60-million overhaul and retrofit. The present service covers some 12 miles (19 km) and utilizes about 40 cars.

Cable car route

⭐ Rather than wait in the long lines at a cable car terminus, do what the locals do and walk up a stop or two, where you can hop on right away – then hold on!

The $2.00 fare is for one ride, one direction only, and there are no transfers. Consider getting a CityPass or a Muni Passport *(see p134).*

• Cable Car Museum: 1201 Mason St, at Washington; Map M3; (415) 474-1887; www.cablecar museum.org; Open Apr–Sep: 10am–6pm daily; Oct–Mar: 10am–5pm daily; Free

Top 10 Features

1. Cars
2. Bell
3. Grip Person
4. Conductor
5. Cables
6. Braking
7. Cable Car Museum
8. Riding Styles
9. Turntables
10. Routes

Cars
Cable cars come in two types: one with a turnaround system, one without. All are numbered, have wood and brass fittings in the 19th-century style, and are often painted in differing colors.

Bell
During the course of operation up and down the busy hills, the cable car's bell *(above)* is used by the grip person like a claxon, to warn other vehicles and pedestrians of imminent stops, starts, and turns.

Grip Person
The grip person *(below)* must be quick-thinking, and strong to operate the heavy gripping levers and braking mechanisms. The grip is like a huge pair of pliers that clamps onto the cable to pull the car along.

 Every grip person develops their own signature ring on the car's bell, and a ringing contest is held every July in Union Square.

Conductor
4 The conductor not only collects fares, but also makes sure that everyone travels safely, and that the grip person has room to do his job.

Cables
5 The underground cables are 1.25 inches (3 cm) in diameter and consist of six steel strands of 19 wires each, wrapped around a rope, which acts as a shock absorber.

Turntables
9 Part of the fun of cable-car lore is being there to watch when the grip person and conductor turn their car around for the return trip. The best view is at Powell and Market streets (left).

Routes
10 The three existing routes cover the Financial District, Nob Hill (below), Chinatown, North Beach, Russian Hill, and Fisherman's Wharf areas. As these are always important destinations for visitors – and for many residents, too – most people find that a cable car ride will be practical as well as pleasurable.

Braking
6 There are three braking mechanisms. Wheel brakes press against the wheels; track brakes press against the tracks when the grip person pulls a lever; while the emergency brake is a steel wedge forced into the rail slot.

Riding Styles
8 There is a choice of sitting inside a glassed-in compartment, sitting on outside wooden benches, or hanging onto poles and standing on the running board (above). The third gives you the sights, sounds, and smells of San Francisco at their most enticing.

Cable Cars and Streetcars

Wire rope manufacturer Andrew Hallidie's cable car system dates from August 2, 1873, when he tested his prototype based on mining cars. It was an immediate success and spawned imitators in more than a dozen cities worldwide. However, 20 years later, the system was set to be replaced by the electric streetcar. Fortunately, resistance to above-ground wires, corruption in City Hall, and finally the 1906 earthquake sidetracked those plans. The cable car was kept for the steepest lines, while the streetcar took over the longer, flatter routes.

Cable Car Museum 7
Downstairs, look at the giant sheaves (wheels), that keep the cables moving throughout the system; upstairs are displays of the earliest cable cars (right).

The cables, which cost at least $20,000 each, must be replaced every two to three months due to the terrific wear and tear.

TOP 10 Fisherman's Wharf

A certain aura of authenticity still clings to San Francisco's old wharf area, but you'll have to look closely to find the historic details – mostly, it has been overwhelmed by tourism. Nevertheless, it's fun to get a walkaway crab cocktail and a chunk of sourdough bread, and to sidestep the crowds to check out the few remaining fishing boats that still haul in their daily bounty. And after all, what's so bad about taking home a few San Francisco souvenirs?

Fisherman's Wharf sign

🍽 Try one of the Wharf's oldest institutions, Scoma's (Pier 47 & Alcona Way; 415 771-4383), for seafood.

• Map J3 • San Francisco Maritime Museum: 900 Beach St; (415) 561-7100; www.nps.gov/safr; Open 10am–5pm daily; Donation
• USS Pampanito: Pier 45 Jefferson St; (415) 775-1943; www. maritime.org; Open Jun–Sep: 9am–8pm daily; Oct–May: 9am–6pm Sun–Thu, 9am–8pm Fri–Sat; Adm $9
• Ripleys Believe It Or Not!: 175 Jefferson St; (415) 771-6188; www. ripleysf.com; Open Labor Day–mid-Jun: 10am–10pm Sun–Thu, 10am–midnight Fri–Sat; Adm $12.95
• Wax Museum: 145 Jefferson St; 1 (800) 439 4305, (415) 202-0402; Open 10am–10pm Mon–Fri, 9am–10:30pm Sat–Sun; Adm $12.95
• Aquarium of the Bay: Embarcadero; 1-888-SEA-DIVE; Open Jun–Aug: 9am–8pm daily; Sep–May: 10am–6pm Mon–Fri, 10am–7pm Sat–Sun; Adm $13.95

Top 10 Sights

1. Ghirardelli Square
2. San Francisco Maritime Museum
3. The Cannery
4. Pier 39
5. USS *Pampanito*
6. Fisherman's and Seaman's Memorial Chapel
7. Fish Alley
8. Aquarium of the Bay
9. Boudin Bakery
10. Ripley's Believe it or Not! and Wax Museum

1 Ghirardelli Square
The Ghirardelli family ran a chocolate factory here from 1859 to 1962. The site *(below)* is now home to upscale shops and eateries *(see pp96–7)*.

2 San Francisco Maritime Museum
Inside you'll find artifacts from the sea-going and fishing culture that made this area famous.

3 The Cannery
A makeover of this former warehouse was completed in 1967, and it's now the site of some appealing boutiques, as well as tourist shops.

4 Pier 39
Built over a disused pier, this 1978 commercial venture became an instant success for promoting tourism in the wharf area *(below)*. Two floors of shops and eateries, with a large central promenade complete with an antique Venetian carousel, keep drawing in the crowds.

Don't miss the pod of wild sea lions that lounge around the docks just to the west of Pier 39.

5 USS Pampanito
This vintage submarine *(above)* sank six enemy ships and damaged four others in World War II. You can tour its interior and get an idea of what life was like for the crew.

Plan of Fisherman's Wharf

9 Boudin Bakery
This is the home of the famous chain of San Francisco sourdough breadmakers. Stop by to try the distinctive crusty round loaf, best enjoyed warm from the oven with plenty of butter.

10 Ripleys Believe It Or Not! and Wax Museum
These two fun-zone denizens *(below)* — found as "attractions" around the world – are a give-away that these blocks of Jefferson Street are pure tourist trap.

6 Fisherman's and Seaman's Memorial Chapel
This little wooden chapel was built in 1980 as an interfaith memorial to all those who make and have made their living at sea.

7 Fish Alley
This alley *(right)* is possibly the last vestige of the authentic, workaday wharf. Here you can see fishing boats come in and watch as the catch of the day is landed and prepared for market.

8 Aquarium of the Bay
The aquarium's trans-parent tunnel visually immerses you in the San Francisco Bay marine habitat, where thousands of members of diverse ocean fauna disport themselves before your eyes. Video presentations and marine specialists help you understand what you're seeing.

The Port of San Francisco
In 1853 the first wharf was built here, and it quickly became a center for maritime-related enterprise, including shipbuilding, and fresh seafood joints. Italians soon monopolized almost every aspect of the fishing industry – even today, most of the eateries along the Wharf bear Italian names. With technology, however, the Bay was fished-out by the 1950s, and any big-time fishing industry went out of business or moved elsewhere.

TOP 10 Alcatraz

To the inmates who were confined on this island prison, in operation from 1934 to 1963, their punishment was not only captivity but also psychological torture. After all, they were right in the midst of one of America's busiest harbors, with small craft darting to and from San Francisco, Oakland, Berkeley, and Sausalito, and they could probably hear the ceaseless procession of automobiles crossing the bridges and honking their horns. They could certainly see the ocean liners as they glided through the Golden Gate to far away ports – all reminding them that life was near, but freedom very far.

View of Alcatraz Island from San Francisco

🖸 Picnicking is allowed on the dock, but you'll have to bring your own food. The visitor center does sell water, however.

🕑 The weather is often blustery and cold on the island, and the trails and walkways rough. Wear warm clothes and strong, comfortable shoes.

The audioguide is well worth the extra few dollars, as is the ranger-guided tour.

• Blue & Gold Fleet Ferries from Pier 41: (415) 705-5555 (tickets and schedules)
• www.nps.gov/alcatraz
• Open daily
• Adm: $16 (day tours); $23.50 (evening tours)

Top 10 Features

1. Lighthouse
2. Cell Block
3. Exercise Yard
4. Control Room
5. D Block
6. Dining Room
7. Chapel
8. Broadway
9. Visitor Center
10. Warden's House

Lighthouse
Alcatraz Island was the site of the very first lighthouse built on the West Coast in 1854. The original lighthouse was replaced in 1909 with an automated one, to tower above the new cell block.

Cell Blocks
The cell house contains four free-standing cell blocks *(below)*. The complex was built by military prisoners in 1911 and was once the largest reinforced concrete building in the world. In all, there were 390 cells, but the population averaged only about 260 at any one time.

Exercise Yard
With a strict "no-talking" rule and the monotonous gloom of being cut off from life, prisoners whose good behavior qualified them for a turn around the walled-in Exercise Yard *(above)* must have felt very relieved. Here they could walk, rather than pace in their cells, where they spent 16 to 23 hours every day.

 You cannot visit Alcatraz independently – booking a guided tour with the ferry company is required.

4 Control Room
From this bunker-like facility, reinforced to withstand siege, the guards controlled the 24-hour electric security system. Next to the Control Room was the visiting area, where thick glass separated prisoners and visitors, and conversations were held over monitored telephones.

5 D Block
Any prisoner who transgressed the strict rules and regulations would be sent to D Block *(above)*, the 42 solitary confinement cells kept entirely without light.

9 Visitor Center
The Visitor Center is located in the old barracks building behind the ferry jetty *(below)*. It houses a bookstore, exhibits, and a multi-media show providing a historical overview of Alcatraz, and an information counter.

10 Warden's House
Until the house burned down in 1970, the warden's home looked out to freedom. Designed in Mission Revival style, the home had 17 large rooms, and sweeping views of the Golden Gate Bridge and San Francisco lights.

The History of "The Rock"
The name "Alcatraz" derives from the Spanish *alcatraces*, for the birds that Spanish explorer Juan Manuel de Ayala observed here when he sailed into the Bay in 1775. In 1850, a presidential order set aside the island for the US Army to build a citadel, but defense became less of a priority and, in 1909, it became a military prison. In 1933 the Federal Government decided to open a maximum-security penitentiary here. Yet Alcatraz was not the "Devil's Island" that many think it was – the conditions, such as one man per cell, were better than other jails.

6 Dining Room
Meals were one of the few things prisoners had to look forward to, and they were generally well-fed, to quell rebellion. Note the sample menu on display at the kitchen entrance.

7 Chapel
On top of the guardhouse, a Mission-style military chapel *(above)* was built during the 1920s. It was used as living quarters and a school, as well as a chapel. During the post-1930s prison phase, the building was used to house prison staff.

8 Broadway
The corridor that separates C and B blocks *(left)* was jokingly nick-named by prisoners after New York City's glittering thoroughfare, famous for its nightlife. The inter-section at the end was named "Times Square."

Left **Al Capone** Right **Scene from the film** *Escape from Alcatraz*

🔟 Stories from The Rock

1 Robert "Birdman" Stroud
The most famous inmate was dubbed the "Birdman", despite the fact that he was not permitted to conduct his avian studies during his 17 years here. Due to his violent nature Stroud spent most of those years in solitary.

2 Birdman of Alcatraz
This 1962 movie presented Stroud as a nature-loving ornithologist, bending historical fact to the service of a good story.

3 Al Capone
In 1934 Capone was among the first "official" shipment of prisoners. The infamous gangster was assigned menial jobs and treated like every other inmate.

4 George "Machine Gun" Kelly
Jailed in 1933 for kidnapping, Kelly was given a life sentence, and was sent to Alcatraz for 17 years. He was considered a model prisoner by the officers.

Robert "Birdman" Stroud

5 Alvin "Creepy" Karpis
Karpis robbed his way through the Midwest between 1931 and 1936, and earned himself the title Public Enemy Number One. He was imprisoned on Alcatraz from 1936 to 1962. He committed suicide in 1979.

6 Morton Sobell
Charged with conspiracy to commit treason, Sobell arrived on Alcatraz in 1952 and spent five years as its most famous political prisoner, being a victim of J. Edgar Hoover's witch hunt for Communist subversives. Once freed, Sobell returned to live in San Francisco, where he still resides today.

7 Anglin Brothers
The brothers, John and Clarence, are notable as the only two known inmates to successfully escape from The Rock.

8 Escape from Alcatraz
Starring Clint Eastwood as one of the Anglin brothers, again, this 1979 film is largely Hollywood fiction. However, the depiction of prison life is reportedly accurate.

9 Frank Wathernam
The last prisoner to leave Alcatraz, on March 21, 1963.

10 The Rock
Hollywood has never lost its fascination with Alcatraz, as can be seen in this 1997 action thriller, starring Sean Connery.

Top10 Escape Attempts

1. December, 1937: Theodore Cole & Ralph Roe
2. May, 1938: James Limerick, Jimmy Lucas, & Rufus Franklin
3. January, 1939: Arthur "Doc" Barker, Dale Stamphill, William Martin, Henry Young, & Rufus McCain
4. May, 1941: Joe Cretzer, Sam Shockley, Arnold Kyle, & Lloyd Barkdoll
5. April, 1943: James Boarman, Harold Brest, Floyd Hamilton, & Fred Hunter
6. July, 1945: John Giles
7. May, 1946: Bernard Coy, Joe Cretzer, Marvin Hubbard, Sam Shockley, Miran Thompson, & Clarence Carnes
8. September, 1958: Aaron Burgett & Clyde Johnson
9. June, 1962: Frank Morris & John and Clarence Anglin
10. December, 1962: John Paul Scott & Darl Parker

Native American Occupation

In 1969 Richard Oakes and 90 Native Americans landed on Alcatraz, set up camp, and demanded the government sell them the island for $24 worth of beads and red cloth. They claimed that this was the price their people had been paid in exchange for an island similar in size nearly 300 years earlier. The government considered forcibly removing the occupiers, but growing public support for the Indians forced officials to renew negotiations. However, in January 1970, while playing on the rooftop of one of the buildings, Oakes' youngest daughter slipped and fell to her death; distraught, he and his family decided to abandon their claim. Sixty Native Americans remained, but as the stalemate dragged on, the majority slowly began to leave – only 15 chose to stay. In June 1970, fires ravaged the warden's house, the recreation hall, the officers' club, and the lighthouse. Following this devastation, government troops staged a pre-dawn raid. The remaining Indians were arrested and the 19-month Indian occupation came to an end.

Liberation Day
One of the occupying Sioux Indians, Fear Forgets, led defiant Liberation Day celebrations on the island on May 31, 1970.

Teepee set up on Alcatraz during the Native American occupation

TOP 10 Chinatown

This teeming, densely populated neighborhood, with its bright façades, noisy markets, exotic temples, and ethnic restaurants and shops, is like a city within the city – and a place every visit to San Francisco must include. The atmosphere recalls a typical southern Chinese town, although the architecture, customs, and public celebrations are distinctly American hybrids on a Cantonese theme. Overlook the tourist tackiness, check out some of the side alleys, and give yourself time to take it all in.

Colorful awning, Chinatown shop

🚗 Don't drive into Chinatown: it's very congested, and parking is impossible. Take the cable car – all three lines will get you there *(see p11)*.

🍽 One of the best Chinese restaurants in town is Tommy Toy's *(see p91)*.

• Map N4
• Golden Gate Fortune Cookies Company: 56 Ross Alley; Map M4;
• Old Chinese Telephone Exchange: Bank of Canton, 743 Washington St; Map M4;
• Tin How Temple: 125 Waverly Place, top floor; Map N4; Open 9am–4pm daily
• Chinese Six Companies: 843 Stockton St; Map N4
• Chinese Historical Society of America Museum and Learning Center: 965 Clay St; Map N5; www.chsa.org
• Chinese Culture Center: Holiday Inn, 750 Kearny St, 3rd floor; Map M5; 986-1822; www.c-c-c.org

Top 10 Sights

1. Chinatown Gate
2. Portsmouth Square
3. Golden Gate Fortune Cookies Company
4. Old Chinese Telephone Exchange
5. Temples
6. Stockton Street Chinese Markets
7. Chinese Six Companies
8. Chinese Historical Society of America Museum and Learning Center
9. Chinese Culture Center
10. St Mary's Square

1 Chinatown Gate
A gift from Taiwan in 1970, this triple-pagoda southern entrance to Chinatown *(above)* was inspired by traditional Chinese village gates.

2 Portsmouth Square
This was San Francisco's original town square – here, on July 9, 1846, the US flag was first raised on the Bay, when the port was seized from Mexico. Locals now use the area for *t'ai chi* and games of *mah-jong*.

3 Golden Gate Fortune Cookies Company
Fortune cookies were invented in San Francisco. Stop by to watch how the skillful workers *(left)* slip the fortune message in the cookie mixture, then fold it into the traditional shapes.

 The finest Chinese antiques shops are found at the Chinatown Gate end of Grant Avenue, just inside the gate.

Old Chinese Telephone Exchange
4 This three-tiered pagoda is now the Bank of Canton, and is the most distinctive work of architectural chinoiserie in Chinatown. It served as the telephone exchange until the 1950s.

Stockton Street Chinese Markets
6 At these authentic produce markets the real smells, sights, and sounds of Chinatown come into sharp focus *(above)*.

Map of Chinatown

Chinese Culture Center
9 The Chinese Culture Center comprises an art gallery and a small crafts shop, featuring the work of Chinese and Chinese-American artists.

St Mary's Square
10 This square is graced by a stainless-steel and rose-granite statue of Sun Yat-sen *(below)* by San Francisco sculptor Beniamino Bufano.

Temples
5 There are a number of temples that incorporate Confucian, Taoist, and Buddhist elements. The Tin How Temple *(below)* was founded in 1852 and dedicated to the Queen of Heaven.

Chinese Six Companies
7 This building's brilliant façade is one of the most ornate in Chinatown. The Six Companies was formed in 1882 to promote Chinese interests within the community.

Chinese Historical Society of America Museum and Learning Center
8 This is the new home for the Chinese Historical Society's 15,000-piece collection of artifacts, documents, photographs, and replicas that illustrate and explain the Chinese-American experience.

Gold Rush Cantonese

Chinese immigrants began to arrive with the Gold Rush, to get rich quick and return home heroes. As it happened, things went politically sour in China at the time, and many Chinese stayed in the new land. Unfortunately, there was a racist backlash against them, resulting in the Chinese Exclusion Act of 1882, and Chinatown became a kind of ghetto, full of opium dens and vice. The Act was repealed in 1943, and things have steadily improved ever since.

The Chinese Culture Center sponsors a lively series of lectures and seminars, as well as walking tours of Chinatown.

🔟 Golden Gate Park

Golden Gate Park is every San Franciscan's beloved backyard. Any weekend finds hundreds of people coming here to play or just to relax and breathe in the heady air. Almost every conceivable sort of recreational activity is available: hiking, running, cycling, golf, tennis, baseball, soccer, fishing, and more. There's also the very first children's playground in the US with the magnificent Herschel-Spillman Carousel, built in 1912 (see p59). Even on a rainy day, the park offers world-class activities in the form of the California Academy of Sciences Natural History Museum, Morrison Planetarium, and, perhaps best of all, the marvelous Steinhart Aquarium (see pp22–3).

Shakespeare Garden entrance

🛈 For information and a map of the park, stop at the McLaren Lodge, originally the home of the park's chief gardener. It is now a visitor center (501 Stanyan St, open 8am–5pm Mon–Fri).

• Entrances on Fulton St, Lincoln Way, Stanyan St & the Great Hwy
• Map D4 • (415) 831-2700 • www.parks.sfgov.org • Open sunrise–sunset daily • Free
• Japanese Tea Garden: Hagiwara Tea Garden Drive; (415) 752 4227; Open Apr–Oct: 9am–6pm daily, Nov–Mar: 8:30am–5pm daily; Adm $3.50
• Strybing Arboretum & Botanical Gardens: 9th Ave at Lincoln Way; Open 8am–4:30pm Mon–Fri, 10am–5pm Sat–Sun; Contribution
• California Academy of Sciences: Music Concourse; www.calacademy.org; Open 10am–5pm daily; Adm $8, planetarium $2.50 extra

Top 10 Sights

1. Hippie Hill
2. Victorian Conservatory of Flowers
3. Giant Tree Fern Grove and John McLaren Rhododendron Dell
4. Music Concourse
5. Japanese Tea Garden
6. Shakespeare Garden
7. Strybing Arboretum and Botanical Gardens
8. Stow Lake and Strawberry Hill
9. Buffalo Paddock
10. Dutch Windmill and Queen Wilhelmina Tulip Garden

1 Hippie Hill

This pleasant slope, a short walk from Haight-Ashbury, was the celebrated site of stoned-out gatherings in the 1960s.

2 Victorian Conservatory of Flowers

The park's oldest building, a copy of London's Kew Gardens (below), shelters more than 20,000 rare and exotic plants.

3 Giant Tree Fern Grove and John McLaren Rhododendron Dell

Coming upon the Giant Tree Fern Grove, with its huge, curling proto-flora gathered around a small central lagoon, is like venturing into a primeval forest. Just a bit farther to the west, the Rhododendron Dell contains the largest array of these gorgeous blooms (850 varieties) of any US garden.

For more parks and gardens **See pp48–9**

Map of Golden Gate Park

Music Concourse
This area provides the cultural focus for the park, dating from 1894. There are free concerts on Sundays and events sponsored by the San Francisco Opera *(see p56)*.

Japanese Tea Garden
This eternally delightful garden is full of refined detail: bonsai trees, rock gardens, exotic plantings, and pagodas *(above)*.

Shakespeare Garden
This charming English garden features the 200-odd flowers, herbs, and such, mentioned in the Bard's works. Bronze plaques quote appropriate passages.

Strybing Arboretum and Botanical Gardens
This vast area is home to more than 7,000 species from countries with climates similar to that of San Francisco. Environments include a Redwood Nature Trail, a Primitive Plant Garden, and a Biblical Garden.

Stow Lake and Strawberry Hill
Strawberry Hill is actually the large island in the middle of this placid lake, which is ideal for boating. Don't miss the elaborate Chinese moon-viewing pavilion on the island's eastern shore, a gift from Taipei in 1981 *(above)*.

Buffalo Paddock
American buffalo were first brought here in 1894. In 1984 a small herd was given a home again, roaming under the eucalyptus trees *(left)*.

Dutch Windmill and Queen Wilhelmina Tulip Garden
The windmill *(above)*, and the tulip garden that surrounds it, were both gifts from the queen of the Netherlands in 1902. The windmill is one of the world's largest and was restored in 1981.

A Miracle of Land Reclamation

The park's more than 1,000 acres are some 3 miles (5 km) long and half a mile (1 km) wide, making it the largest cultivated urban park in the US. There are 27 miles (43 km) of footpaths, winding through gardens, lakes, waterfalls, and forests. But it was not always so. Before the 1870s the entire area was sandy wastes and scrubland. William Hammond Hall made great progress over two decades, then hired Scottish gardener John McLaren in 1890. "Uncle John", as he was known, made the park his life's work, devoting himself to its perfection until his death in 1943, at the age of 97.

The Garden of Fragrance in the Strybing Arboretum is specially designed for the visually impaired to enjoy.

Left **California Academy of Sciences façade** Right **Fish Roundabout**

California Academy of Sciences

1 Steinhart Aquarium
More than 14,000 specimens of mollusks, sea mammals, sharks and other fish dwell in one of the world's largest aquariums, and the oldest in the US. Some 200 displays feature the diversity of aquatic life, from the oddest fish in the world, such as the turkey fish, to the most threatening, such as piranhas.

2 Fish Roundabout
Spiraling upward, this is a circular viewing area populated with varieties of saltwater species, including California barracuda, Pacific bonito and mackerel, yellowtail jack, and ocean whitefish.

3 Touch Tidepool
Shake hands with a starfish, get cozy with hermit crabs, or pick up a sea slug in this hands-on, hands-wet attraction. The pool is staffed by volunteers who will tell you what you're handling and keep the animals safe, too. Hours vary, since the creatures get a much deserved time-out from time to time.

4 Penguin Feeding Time
These Black-footed penguins are fed twice daily, at 11:30am and 4pm, and it's always a spectacle that the whole family enjoys. Penguins may waddle on land, but their grace is evident when you see them dive and glide effortlessly through the water to catch their meal.

5 Natural History Museum
The academy features multimedia exhibits, excellent dioramas of animals in their natural habitats, human artifacts from various world cultures, the Hall of Fossils, the Gem and Mineral Hall, an insect room, and hilarious *Far Side of Science* cartoons by Gary Larson.

6 Life Through Time
This is a 3.5 billion-year journey through the development of life on Earth. Discover, partly through the use of interactive computers, how evolutionary trends arose over time and how certain species evolved. There are also exhibits such as life-size dinosaur models, a huge T-Rex tooth, giant flightless birds, and other mind-boggling scenes from Earth's remote past.

Touch Tidepool

 From 2004–8 the museum is being renovated and is moving to a temporary home at 875 Howard St. For details: www.calacademy.org

7 Earthquake!

This exhibit sheds light on one of Earth's most fascinating and terrifying natural phenomena – and one that San Franciscans know all too well. The main attraction is a multimedia theater that allows you to experience a tremor first-hand. It also features survivor accounts and actual video footage of past earthquakes – plus pointers on how to prepare for the real thing (see p139).

8 Wild California

The huge diversity of California's ecosystems is beautifully explored in this section of the museum. By means of superb dioramas all the landscapes and wildlife of the state are portrayed. Everything is investigated in captivating ways, from rocky cliffs populated by giant elephant seals, to magnified insect life, to the microscopic goings-on in a typical pocket of the Pacific Ocean waters.

California Academy of Sciences Floorplan

9 African Hall

Magnificent dioramas show African fauna, such as cheetahs, rhinos, lions, giraffes, and the straight-horned oryx in their natural surroundings. The exhibit ends with the African Waterhole, which features on-location recordings of bird and animal sounds and a 17-minute simulation of a 24-hour cycle in Africa.

10 Morrison Planetarium

Take a guided tour of the universe. The night skies never looked more real, and you can travel to the very limits of the known universe. Shows are presented Monday to Friday at 2pm, and weekends on the hour from noon to 4pm.

Earthquake! diorama

🔟 Grace Cathedral

Inspired by Notre Dame in Paris, the third largest Episcopal cathedral in the US stands on the site of Charles Crocker's Nob Hill mansion, which was destroyed in the 1906 disaster. Work began on it in 1910 but was not finally completed until 1964. It is constructed of steel and concrete, despite its Gothic look, so as to withstand the city's seismic vagaries. The interior is replete with marble and abundant stained glass, and other sumptuous touches both within and without make it one of America's most lavish religious structures.

Façade

🔵 The cathedral has a simple café, located downstairs on the north side of Cathedral Close, along with a shop.

🕐 Visit the cathedral during Thursday Evensong (usually at 5:15pm), when the lighting is at its most dramatic.

• 1100 California St
• Map N3
• (415) 749-6300
• www.gracecathedral.org
• Open 7am–6pm Sun–Fri, 8am–6pm Sat
• Free

Top 10 Features

1. Carillon Tower
2. Rose Window
3. Chapel of Grace
4. Doors of Paradise
5. New Testament Window
6. 20th-Century Windows
7. Keith Haring's Altarpiece
8. The Organ
9. Marble Labyrinth
10. Maze & Bufano St. Francis of Assisi

1 Carillon Tower

The belfry contains a carillon of 44 bronze bells, cast in England in 1938. The bourdon bell, which tolls the hour, is the largest European-style bell in the US. Many of the bells have evocative names, such as Loving Kindness, and Joy to the World.

2 Rose Window

This 25-ft (8-m) work of faceted glass *(below)* symbolizes the themes of the Canticle of the Sun, a famous devotional poem written by St. Francis of Assisi.

3 Chapel of Grace

This chapel *(above)* was the first completed unit of the cathedral (1930). Its architecture, windows, and apse mural were inspired by the royal Sainte Chapelle in Paris. Its furnishings are a mix of ages and origins, including the medieval French stone altar, the 17th-century German altar cross, the English Gothic prayer desk, and the painting of the Madonna and Child inspired by Italian Renaissance artist Giovanni Bellini.

 The Chapel of Grace seats 120 people and is used for daily services, weddings, and special events.

4 Doors of Paradise
The cathedral doors *(left)* are bronze and gold plate replicas of the ones made for the Baptistry in Florence, Italy. The 10 panels depict Old Testament stories, beginning at the top left with Adam and Eve.

7 Keith Haring's Altarpiece
The AIDS Interfaith Memorial Chapel contains a triptych altarpiece of bronze and white gold *(below)* by the New York artist Keith Haring. It was completed shortly before his own death from AIDS. The central panel shows a multi-armed figure of compassion, while the side panels depict winged souls soaring above.

8 The Organ
This monumental organ dates from 1934. The carved English oak organ screens show angelic musicians, songbirds, and dragons, as well as the instruments of Christ's Passion in the lower portions.

9 Marble Labyrinth
The Interfaith Outdoor Labyrinth is a replica of the one at Chartres Cathedral in France. Such labyrinths were used in medieval times to mimic the arduous pilgrimage to Jerusalem; this practice has recently been revived.

Floorplan of Grace Cathedral

10 Maze and Bufano St. Francis of Assisi
Just beyond the entrance is another floor labyrinth, and an appealing statue of St. Francis of Assisi *(above)* by the late San Franciscan sculptor Beniamino Bufano.

Nob Hill
"Nob" was one of the kinder names reserved for the unscrupulous entrepreneurs who built their mansions on this, San Francisco's highest hill *(see p83)*. Some say the name derives from "nabob", the title for a provincial potentate in India; others say it's simply a contraction of "snob", a theory that would also seem plausible. Despite the loss of almost all of the mansions in the 1906 earthquake, the hill's poshness remains, as home to the city's most celebrated luxury hotels.

5 New Testament Window
The theme of this window is brotherhood and the church. Christ stands with a welcoming gesture, with His disciples flanking.

6 20th-Century Windows
The theme of these windows is human endeavor and they depict creative 20th-century Americans, including physicist Albert Einstein, and astronaut John Glenn.

🔟 San Francisco Museum of Modern Art

Founded in 1935, the SFMOMA is the only museum in the western US devoted to collecting and exhibiting the full scope of modern and contemporary art, and second only to New York's MOMA. The landmark museum moved to its wonderful Post-Modernist setting in the burgeoning South of Market neighborhood (see p29) in January 1995. Its permanent collections include major works by the most important 20th-century European and American artists, extensive photography holdings, and challenging multimedia installations.

Museum façade

🍴 The museum's Caffè Museo (415) 357-4500) features Mediterranean-style snacks and sandwiches.

🎫 Free gallery tours are offered hourly from 11:30am–2:30pm, and at 6:15pm and 7:15pm on Thursdays. Meet in the Atrium.

- 151 3rd St
- Map Q5
- (415) 357-4000
- www.sfmoma.org
- Open 11am–5:45pm Fri–Tue; 11am–8:45pm Thu
- Dis. access
- Adm $12.50; audio tour price varies; free first Tue of month

Top 10 Features

1. Exterior
2. Atrium
3. 20th-Century European Artists
4. 20th-Century American Artists
5. Bay Area Artists
6. Latin American Artists
7. Photography
8. Electronic & Digital Art
9. Temporary Exhibitions
10. The Catwalk

Key

- First floor
- Second floor
- Third floor
- Fourth floor
- Fifth floor

Exterior 1
The building was designed by renowned Swiss architect Mario Botta. The 125-ft (38-m) truncated cylindrical turret *(right)* is decorated with Art Deco-style chevrons.

Atrium 2
The atrium is illuminated by the central skylight and takes in the full height of the building. It acts as a dramatic entrance and public space, hung with two vast, brightly engaging Sol Le Witt geometric paintings *(above)*.

Entrance

The SFMOMA regularly rotates its collections so not all the artworks mentioned may be on display at the time of your visit.

3 20th-Century European Artists

These works are located on the second floor. Here you will find important works by Matisse, Miró, Degas, Picasso, Braque, Klee, Mondrian, Duchamp, Dalí, and Magritte, among others.

5 Bay Area Artists

San Francisco Bay Area artists are also represented on the second floor, and include Richard Diebenkorn, Wayne Thiebaud, and Clyfford Still, all with international reputations. Bay Area figurative painters in the collection include Elmer Bishoff, and David Park. Most noteworthy, perhaps, is *California Artist* (1982), a humorous sculptural self-portrait by Robert Arneson in glazed stoneware *(right)*.

6 Latin American Artists

Latin American art is represented most forcefully by the work of muralist Diego Rivera and his wife Frida Kahlo. Other Latin American painters represented include Wilfredo Lam, and Joaquín Torres-Garcia.

9 Temporary Exhibitions

The museum's temporary exhibition spaces may include educational programs, interactive programs, or retrospective exhibitions of the work of contemporary artists such as Yoko Ono and Eva Hess, or the photography of Victorian author Lewis Carroll.

10 The Catwalk

Suspended high up inside the cylindrical turret, visitors can walk the see-through 35-ft (10-m) steel bridge that cuts across the skylight *(left)*, providing dramatic views of the Sculpture Terrace and the Atrium.

7 Photography

One of the museum's strengths, rotating exhibits may include masterpieces by Man Ray and Ansel Adams, as well as more avant-garde works.

8 Electronic & Digital Art

Established in 1987, the collection includes multimedia works, moving-image pieces, and video installations by such artists as Brian Eno, Bill Viola, Dara Birnbaum, Matthew Barney, and Nam June Paik.

4 20th-Century American Artists

US artists included here are O'Keeffe, de Kooning, Pollock, Warhol, and Kline. One of the perennial hits of the collection *(above)* is Jeff Koons' hilarious ceramic sculpture *Michael Jackson and Bubbles* (1988).

Museum Guide

The MuseumStore, the Caffè Museo, and the Wattis Theater are all on the first floor. The second floor is the main event for most visitors, with paintings and sculptures from the permanent collection, as well as exhibits relating to architecture and design. The third floor focuses on photography and other works on paper, while media arts are on the fourth. Special and temporary exhibitions may be displayed on any of the floors.

Kids love the Koret Visitor Education Center, on the second floor, where there are multimedia displays and art activities.

Left **Aerial view, the Esplanade** Right **Yerba Buena Center for the Arts Theater**

Top 10 Yerba Buena Gardens' Features

1 Yerba Buena Center for the Arts Gallery

Changing exhibitions here explore issues of race, class, gender, history, technology, and art itself. There are temporary exhibitions. ⬡ *701 Mission St • Map Q5 • Open noon–8pm Tue, Wed, Fri, Sat, Sun • Dis. access • Adm • www.ybca.org*

Map of Yerba Buena Gardens

2 Yerba Buena Center for the Arts Theater

Multiculturalism is again the keynote in this 750-seat indoor theater. Performances may range from world-music festivals to Victorian operetta.

3 Moscone Center

Completed in 1981, this was the building that began the renovation of the SoMa district. It was the site of the Democratic Party's convention in 1984. Most of it is underground; above ground the impression is of glass, girders, and gardens. ⬡ *Howard St • Map Q5*

Moscone Center

4 Esplanade

The Esplanade comprises garden-lined walkways, an inviting lawn, rolling hills, trees, and interesting sculptures. Free weekly concert during the summer festival *(www.ybae.org)*.

5 Rooftop Children's Center and Carousel

Located atop the west wing of the Moscone Center, this complex is all about children. The carousel dates from 1906. There's also an ice-skating rink, a bowling center, a learning garden, and an amphitheater. ⬡ *750 Folsom St • Map Q5*

6 Martin Luther King, Jr. Memorial

Featuring words of peace in several languages, this multi-faceted monument incorporates sculpture, a waterfall, and quotations from the Civil Rights leader's speeches and writings.

7 Zeum

This place aims to inspire creative impulses in children – Toyz is a discovery program for new technological applications; the Production Lab gives you the opportunity to produce your own film. Plus there's always an exhibition on. ⬡ *221 4th St • Map Q5 • Open 11am–5pm Wed–Sun • Dis. access • Adm • www.zeum.org*

8 California Historical Society Museum

The state's official historical research organization holds vast collections of photos, books, manuscripts, maps, and fine and decorative arts. Some of the artifacts date as far back as the 1600s. ◎ *678 Mission Street • Map P5 • Open 11am–5pm Tue–Sat • Adm*

9 Mexican Museum and Contemporary Jewish Museum (CJM)

Both of these museums, which chronicle the place of their respective cultures in the weave of life are set to move to new, permanent homes in the Yerba Buena complex. The Mexican Museum opens in 2007 and the CJM in 2008. Check their websites for the most up-to-date information. • *www.mexicanmuseum. org • www.thecjm.org*

10 Metreon

Sony has created an alternative high-tech fun-zone for the city's youth. Its main attraction is a state-of-the-art cineplex, where you can take in the very latest movies' special effects in all their glory. Elsewhere, kids sit in vast darkened rooms and play the latest multimedia games. On the upper deck is a pleasant terrace with a café. ◎ *101 4th St • Map Q4*

Top 10 New Constructions South of Market

1. Pacific Bell Park
2. SFMOMA
3. Moscone Center
4. Yerba Buena Center
5. Rincon Center
6. Metreon
7. South Park
8. The Galleria
9. Ed Hardy San Francisco
10. The Four Seasons and the Marriott hotels

The Rise of South of Market

Formerly a doggedly industrial area full of warehouses and factories, this flat stretch attracted few residents. For nearly 100 years, it was considered unattractive, if not downright dangerous. All that began to change in the 1970s, when slums were cleared away and the Moscone Center was built. Upscale interior designer showrooms soon followed, ensuing decades brought premier nightclubs, and, more recently, the digital boom added more than virtual life to the place. Public structures have sprung up lately, and the whole district is now seen as a desirable neighborhood – at least for creative types.

Esplanade, South of Market

TOP 10 Mission Dolores

The old Misión San Francisco de Asís acquired its popular name, Mission Dolores, from a small stream that once flowed nearby, Arroyo de Nuestra Señora de los Dolores. It is the oldest building in the city of San Francisco and the only intact mission chapel in the chain of 21 (of which it was the sixth) established under the direction of Franciscan friar Father Junipero Serra. The site was consecrated in 1776, and the chapel was built in 1782–91, with the labor of Ohlone Indians. Its adobe walls are 4 ft (1.2 m) thick and its red-tile roofs are typical of the "Mission Style" which can be seen all over California in both old and new buildings. Reportedly, 36,000 handmade and sun-dried adobe bricks were needed to complete the structure.

Chapel and Basilica façades

🅾 For a fresh, authentic taste of Mexico, head for Pancho Villa Taqueria *(see p113).*

✪ Check out the old photos in the covered walkway on the right side of the chapel, which depict, among other things, early Indian festivals and the total destruction in 1906 of the church next door, which was replaced by the basilica.

• 3321 16th St at Dolores St
• Map F5
• (415) 621-8203
• www.missiondolores. citysearch.com
• Open 9am–4pm daily
• Dis. access
• Suggested donation $5 adult, $3 child; 40 minute audio tour in English $5

Top 10 Features

1 Cemetery and Serra Statue
2 Chapel
3 Altarpieces
4 Beamed Ceiling Decoration
5 Diorama and Museum
6 Mission Façade
7 Sorrows of Mary Panels
8 Choir Windows of St Francis
9 Dolores Street
10 Dolores Park

1 Cemetery and Serra Statue

This leafy, picturesque cemetery *(above)* is a gently contemplative place. Many of San Francisco's early leaders are buried here. Central to the space is a life-size sculpture of Father Junipero Serra.

2 Chapel

The central building *(right)* still retains the original redwood beams, lashed together with raw-hide. The amber-colored window glass gives the interior warmth, reflected off gold-leafed fixtures.

3 Altarpieces

The hand-carved, gilded and painted wooden reredos and side altars *(above)* were brought from Mexico in the late 1700s and early 1800s.

For more churches in the city See pp44–5

4 Beamed Ceiling Decoration
The imaginative painted ceiling design derives from Ohlone basketry.

5 Diorama and Museum
Just outside the chapel is a diorama showing what life was like at the mission 200 years ago. A small museum at the back of the chapel contains documents that pertain to the mission's history.

7 Sorrows of Mary Panels
These images along the front of each of two side balconies in the basilica detail the seven moments when Mary was overcome with sorrow *(above)*.

8 Choir Windows of St Francis
At the rear of the basilica, jewel-like stained-glass windows depict scenes from the life of Saint Francis of Assisi, revolutionary patron saint of San Francisco. The lower side windows depict the 21 California Missions.

9 Dolores Street
Undulating like a rollercoaster, this is one of the loveliest streets in San Francisco. Palm trees grace its center all the way along *(above)*.

Mission Façade 6
The modest white façade of the chapel *(right)* is typical of the Mission Style. Its four columns support niches for three bronze bells, which are inscribed with their names and dates. They were added to the mission in the late 18th century.

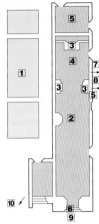

Plan of Mission Dolores

10 Dolores Park
One of the few large green spaces in the Mission District, this park is situated high on a hill and affords excellent views of the city. It was originally the site of San Francisco's main Jewish cemetery, but was transformed in 1905.

Junipero Serra and California's Missions

In 1769, Gaspar de Portola led an expedition to establish missions in California, in the company of Father Junipero Serra and 60 men. They founded Mission San Diego, and then worked their way up to Monterey. Continuing up the coast, within seven years Father Serra had established a mission in San Francisco, with the assistance of Father Francisco Palou. In all, Serra founded 21 missions in Upper and Lower California, many of which survive.

Note: Dolores Park is popular during the day, but at night it can become a connection point for drug dealers.

31

TOP 10 The Wine Country

The world-famous Wine Country comprises two picturesque valleys, Napa and Sonoma, and the extensive hills and dales surrounding them. Altogether, this bucolic zone boasts over 300 wineries, from which countless award-winning wines have emerged. Napa, the slightly more distant of the two, is more developed for visitors, while Sonoma is more low-key but equally inviting. Both are convenient for a day trip, but it's worth spending a day or two here – not only to sample the fruit of the vine but also to take a dip in one of the rejuvenating hot springs that abound throughout the area (see pp34–5).

Napa Valley sign

For very special snacks try the Model Bakery at 1357 Main Street in St Helena.

• Napa Valley Wine Train: 1275 McKinstry St, Napa; (707) 253-2111; www.winetrain.com
• Clos Pegase: 1060 Dunaweal Lane; (707) 942-4981; www.clospegase.com
• Sterling Vineyard: 1111 Dunaweal Lane; (800) 726-6136; www.sterlingvineyards.com
• Opus One: 7900 St Helena Hwy; (707) 944-9442; www.opusonewinery.com
• Domaine Chandon: 1 California Drive, Yountville; (707) 944-8844; www.chandon.com
• Hess Collection: 4411 Redwood Rd, Napa; (707) 255-1144; www.hesscollection.com
• V Sattui: 1111 White Lane, St Helena; (707) 963-7774; www.vsattui.com • Beringer Vineyards: 2000 Main St, St Helena; (707) 963-4812; www.beringer.com • "Old Faithful" Geyser: 1299 Tubbs Lane, Calistoga; (707) 942-6463; Adm $8; www.oldfaithfulgeyser.com

Top 10 Sights
1. Napa Valley Train
2. Sonoma
3. Clos Pegase
4. Sterling Vineyard
5. Opus One
6. Domaine Chandon
7. Hess Collection
8. V Sattui
9. Beringer Vineyards
10. "Old Faithful" Geyser

1 Napa Valley Train
Leaving from Napa and arriving in St. Helena, or vice versa, you can avoid the traffic and partake of a gourmet meal complemented by local wines. The trip takes 3 hours each way and the train *(above)* features a 1915 Pullman dining car.

2 Sonoma
This appealing town, nestled in the Valley of the Moon *(right)*, is filled with high-end restaurants, small hotels, and shops. The town also features a State Historic Park with a mission building and structures from the early to mid-1800s.

3 Clos Pegase
Housed in an award-winning Postmodern structure, this beguiling winery offers free tours and features an extensive collection of modern art. The wine is memorable, too – specialties include Cabernet, Merlot, and Petite Syrah port.

The Napa Valley Wine Train costs $35 each way, but for the gourmet meal the cost rises to $85–$100.

4 Sterling Vineyard
These whitewashed buildings perched on top of a mountain *(above)* can be seen for miles. The self-guided tour is well marked. Notable wines include Cabernet Sauvignon and Merlot.

7 Hess Collection
The tours here are a pleasure, including not only wine-making facilities but also the owner's private art gallery of contemporary European and American artists. The Cabernet Sauvignon, Merlot and Chardonnay are especially good.

Map of the Wine Country

10 "Old Faithful" Geyser
One of only three known geysers in the world that erupt with near-perfect regularity *(below)*. Every 40 minutes, it spews boiling water 60 ft (18 m) into the air.

5 Opus One
Legendary winemaker Robert Mondavi and Baron Philippe de Rothschild have put their skills together to produce Bordeaux-style reds in their state-of-the-art facilities, modeled on the Château Mouton Rothschild winery in France.

6 Domaine Chandon
Lovely gardens, a fine restaurant, and sweeping views complement the sparkling, champagne-style wines of this Moët Hennessy showcase. The winery produces 500,000 cases every year.

8 V Sattui
Extensive gardens *(above)* and a gourmet deli make this the ideal place along the main Napa Valley road to stop for a picnic. Also on offer are wine-tastings of lesser products free of charge – you have to pay for reserve tastings.

9 Beringer Vineyards
The oldest Napa Valley winery, established in 1876, and the most beautiful. Tours include a visit to the 1,000-ft (300-m) wine tunnels, which Chinese laborers carved out of volcanic stone.

California Wine

Since 1857, wine-making has been the mainstay of this area. A phylloxera blight in the early 1900s nearly put an end to it all, but Europe was hit harder, and it was resistant California vines that brought back the wine business to parts of Italy, France, and Spain. In 1976 California wines were put on the international map, when they trounced France in a blind taste-test in Paris. Now, many European producers have wineries in the valley.

Left **Massage treatment** Right **Indian Springs**

🔟 Wine Country Spas

1 Indian Springs
Indian Springs' tradition of purification and healing began over 8,000 years ago, when Native Americans built sweat lodges here over escaping steam. The ancient tradition continues in the historic 1913 bathhouse, restored to pristine condition. Inside, thermal geysers warm volcanic ash in mud baths, and soothing music is played in the treatment rooms. *1712 Lincoln Ave, Calistoga • (707) 942-4913 • www.indianspringscalistoga.com*

2 Calistoga Spa Hot Springs
The motel-like Hot Springs provides a setting in which you can make your visit as restful or as active as you like. Facilities include four outdoor mineral water pools, and exercise and aerobics rooms. *1006 Washington St, Calistoga • (707) 942-6269 • www.calistogaspa.com*

Calistoga Spa Hot Springs

3 Mount View Hotel & Spa
A stay in this historic 1917 resort offers various relaxation and rejuvenation possibilities – mud, milk, or herbal baths, aromatherapy steam showers, body-wraps, massages, or facials – geared to individuals or couples. *1457 Lincoln Ave, Calistoga • (707) 942-5789 • www.mountviewhotel.com*

4 Health Spa Napa Valley
In a serene, open-air setting, guests can yield aches and anxiety to a plethora of pampering and invigorating rituals. For some, that may mean a stimulating fitness workout, or a relaxing grapeseed mud-wrap and massage overlooking the tranquil Spa Garden. *1030 Main St, St Helena • (707) 967-8800 • www.napavalleyspa.com*

5 Dr. Wilkinson's Hot Springs
Over half a century of mud and magic are celebrated here. A mud bath consists of volcanic ash, imported peat, and naturally boiling hot-spring water from the source. Designed for maximum heat penetration and buoyancy, this formula is one of Calistoga's most efficacious. The experience lasts from 10 to 12 minutes and is followed by a warm, mineral water shower. Next comes an aromatic bath, then a steam room. A blanket-wrap follows, then a nap and slow cool down. *1507 Lincoln Ave, Calistoga • (707) 942-4102 • www.drwilkinson.com*

watsu and other massages from certified therapists, attend workshops, and hike throughout the 1,700 acres of land. Or, of course, you can simply lie back and relax. 🔗 *Harbin Springs Rd, north of Middletown • (707) 987-2477 • www.harbin.org*

Fairmont Sonoma Mission Inn & Spa

6 Fairmont Sonoma Mission Inn & Spa

This famous inn provides an oasis of ultimate indulgence in luxury and refinement. Blessed by natural mineral hot springs, the legendary spa, with inspired architecture and plants, is all about understated opulence and serenity. 🔗 *100 Boyes Blvd, Boyes Hot Springs • (707) 938-9000 • www.sonomamissioninn.org*

7 The Kenwood Inn and Spa

Nationally acclaimed as one of the Wine Country's most elegant and intimate country inns, the Kenwood consists of 12 guest suites and a full service spa facility. The inn has the ambiance of an Italian country villa in the heart of the Sonoma Valley, situated on a secluded hillside facing over 1,000 acres of vineyards. The spa offers a variety of massage styles, including aromatherapy and Ayurvedic. 🔗 *10400 Sonoma Hwy, Kenwood • (707) 833-1293 • www.kenwoodinn.com*

8 Harbin Hot Springs

Harbin Hot Springs is a non-profit retreat and workshop center located to the north of Calistoga. Its alternative clientele travel from around the world to soak in the natural spring pools, bask on sun decks, receive

9 Retreat Resort

Located in the beautiful Russian River area, this peaceful setting in the Sonoma County Redwoods offers a reinvigorating retreat from modern life. Body treatments include the Sonoma Salt Glow, Moor Mud Wrap, Desert Heat Body Wrap, Body Polish, Aromatherapy Cocoon, Retreat Wrap, and the Anti-Stress Back Treatment, each lasting approximately one hour. Included in your stay are exclusive use of the pool, Jacuzzi and private meadow, and evening wine-tastings on selected weekends. 🔗 *14711 Armstrong Woods Rd, Guerneville • (707) 869-2706 • www.retreatresort.biz*

10 Sonoma Coast Villa

This family-run, bed and breakfast hotel is nestled in the rolling Californian hills. The Mediterranean-style house is located in 60 acres of beautiful pasturelands near Bodega Bay. Accommodation consists of 16 luxurious rooms with marble bathrooms, fireplaces, and private patios. This secluded retreat offers a variety of spa treatments, including massages, reflexology, and aromatherapy. The hotel can recommend more strenuous activities in the area. 🔗 *16702 Coast Hwy 1, Bodega • (707) 876-9818 • www.scvilla.com*

Left **The Gold Rush** Right **Native Americans**

🔟 Moments in History

1 Native Americans
There were settlements in the Bay as early as the 11th century BC, made up of hunters and gatherers who enjoyed a rich diet of seeds, shellfish, and game. Historians group these peoples into the Coast Miwok, the Wintun, and the Ohlone.

2 Sir Francis Drake
In 1579, the English privateer landed near Point Reyes and claimed Alta California for Queen Elizabeth I. Along with other early explorers of the area, he failed to notice the marvelous bay just inside the straits. England didn't follow up its claim to Northern California, leaving it to the Spanish to conquer.

3 Spanish Control
About 200 years after Drake's wanderings, Spain got serious about establishing a presence in Alta California. In

Statue of Father Junipero Serra

1776, an expedition led by Juan Bautista de Anza arrived at San Francisco Bay and established the Presidio (fort). A mission was also founded by Father Junipero Serra *(see pp30–31)*.

4 American Takeover
Impending war with Mexico in the 1840s inspired US leaders to arouse the interest of Bay Area settlers in joining the Union. In 1846, a party of Yankees in Sonoma declared California's independence from Mexico, christening it the Bear Flag Republic. Shortly after, Commodore John Sloat claimed California as US territory.

5 Gold Rush Days
In 1848 landowner John Sutter noticed a curious glitter in the sediment of the American River in the Sierra Nevada foothills and realized it was gold. Despite attempts to keep the discovery quiet, word leaked out, and businessman Sam Brannan displayed a bottle of gold dust and nuggets for the whole city to see. The subsequent stampede of '49ers turned the city into a boom town overnight.

6 Wells Fargo
Stagecoaches of Wells Fargo & Co began carrying freight and passengers in 1852, taking full advantage of the momentum set up by the Gold Rush. It was also instrumental in the development of the Pony Express *(see p41)*.

7 Panama-Pacific Exposition
Held in 1915 to celebrate the opening of the Panama Canal, the real *raison d'être* for the festivities was that San Franciscans had resurrected their city after the 1906 disaster *(see p94)*.

8 Bay and Golden Gate Bridges
The Bay Bridge's inauguration in 1936 heralded the end of the age of ferryboats by linking the city to the East Bay. The inauguration of the Golden Gate Bridge took place a year later *(see pp8–9)*.

Hippie reveller, Summer of Love

9 "Summer of Love"
San Francisco counterculture burst forth in the summer of 1967. Suddenly, hippies were everywhere, and the eerie, poetic music that embodied a new way of thinking filled the air. It was a socio-political shift that affected the whole world.

10 Senators Feinstein and Boxer
California has always been several steps ahead of the rest of the country. In 1992 it became the first state to send two women Senators to the US Congress, Dianne Feinstein and Barbara Boxer.

Top 10 Scandals and Disasters

1 Native Americans' Near-Extinction
In the late 1800s Native Americans were hunted down by settlers, with a bounty paid for each scalp.

2 Gold Rush Lawlessness
Gold Rush frontier life was so criminal that vigilante justice was proclaimed in the 1850s, leading to secret trials.

3 1906
The earthquake and consequent fire devastated much of the city, and 250,000 people were left homeless.

4 "Bloody Thursday"
On July 5, 1934, police fired shots at striking longshoremen, leaving two dead.

5 Howl
On October 13, 1955, Allen Ginsberg read his revolutionary poem in San Francisco, which was later banned as obscene.

6 Freedom & Anti-War
Pro-Civil Rights and anti-Vietnam War riots occurred from 1964 to 1970

7 Rock Icons Die
Part of hippie legend, Janis Joplin and Jimi Hendrix died of heroin overdoses in 1970.

8 White's Revenge
In 1978 ex-Supervisor Dan White shot dead Mayor George Moscone and gay Supervisor Harvey Milk *(see p39)*.

9 AIDS
The AIDS epidemic reached overwhelming proportions in the city in the 1980s.

10 Loma Prieta Earthquake
In October 1989, the quake destroyed the Victorian center of Santa Cruz *(see p78)* and part of the Bay Bridge.

Left **Fairmont Hotel, Nob Hill** Center **City Hall** Right **Intersection, Haight-Ashbury**

🔟 Historic Sites

1 Mission Dolores
The 18th-century Spanish mission, site of the area's earliest settlement, is worth a visit for its tranquility, as well as for the education it provides about the city's early history *(see pp30–31)*.

2 Jackson Square
The area that witnessed the worst misbehavior of the Barbary Coast days contains some of the city's oldest, loveliest buildings. One of the very few areas that were spared in the 1906 conflagration *(see p84)*.

3 Nob Hill
Erstwhile site of the mansions of Golden Age moguls and potentates, from these lofty heights now rise the city's most lavish hotels and the Gothic spires of one of its best-loved cathedrals *(see p83)*.

Jackson Square

4 Fisherman's Wharf
Remnants of the early fishing industry that contributed to San Francisco's growth are still found here, just layered over with a slick veneer of tourism. Fishing boats still come in and deliver their catch of the day, and nature makes its presence known with a colony of sea lions that lounge on the pier *(see pp12–13)*.

5 War Memorial Opera House
This building was inaugurated in 1932 with a performance of Puccini's *Tosca*, giving the art form a permanent home here. Modeled on its European forbears, with a marble lobby, huge chandelier, balconies, and vaulted ceilings, it is dedicated to the memory of World War I soldiers. In 1945 the Opera House hosted the plenary sessions that preceded the founding of the United Nations and, in 1951, it was the site of the signing of the peace treaty between the US and Japan *(see p56)*.

6 North Beach
The entire area resonates with the history of the early Italian residents, but even more with the iconoclastic legacy of the revolutionary Beats, who brought the neighborhood worldwide fame. Historic churches stand as clear landmarks, while equally historic saloons and cafés take a little snooping around to find *(see p83)*.

For more moments in San Francisco's history **See pp36–7**

Café sign, Haight-Ashbury

7 Haight-Ashbury
The matrix of yet another Bohemian movement that San Francisco has given birth to, this area nurtured idealistic hippies in the late 1960s. They brought international awareness to alternative ways of life, living in harmony with nature and espousing humane values *(see p108)*.

8 Fillmore Auditorium
One of the legendary homes of psychedelic rock during the 1960s. Along with the Avalon Ballroom and the Winterland (both now gone), this is where the San Francisco Sound found its first audience. ® *1805 Geary Blvd • Map E3*

9 City Hall
On November 28, 1978, ex-Supervisor Dan White went to City Hall and assassinated Mayor George Moscone and gay Supervisor Harvey Milk *(see p37)*. In a botched trial, he was convicted of manslaughter, sparking riots from the gay community *(see p84)*.
® *1 Dr. Carlton B. Goodlett Place • Map R1*

10 Sutro Baths
Built in 1896 by silver magnate Adolph Sutro, these were at one time the world's largest heated swimming pools, over-arched by a stunning glass roof. The complex was destroyed by fire in 1966, but you can access the ruins by steps at the Merrie Way parking lot *(see p116)*.

Top 10 Historic Figures

1 Junipero Serra
This 18th-century Spanish cleric traveled up and down California establishing missions, including Mission Dolores *(see p31)*.

2 John C. Fremont
Instrumental in the US annexation of California in the mid-1800s, it was Fremont who dubbed the Bay straits the "Golden Gate".

3 John Muir
Muir was a keen promoter of the National Parks movement. The Muir Woods are named in his honor *(see p78)*.

4 Leland Stanford
One of the "Big Four" who masterminded the Transcontinental railroad also founded Stanford University *(see p125)*.

5 Mark Hopkins
Another of the "Big Four" who struck it super-rich and lived on Nob Hill.

6 Charles Crocker
Another "Big Four" accomplice. The Crocker Galleria recalls his legacy *(see p50–51)*.

7 A.P. Giannini
Founder in 1904 of the Bank of Italy, later the Bank of America, Giannini financed the Golden Gate Bridge.

8 Harvey Milk
The first openly gay politician to become a member of the Board of Supervisors was assassinated in 1978.

9 Dianne Feinstein
One of the movers and shakers of San Francisco politics in recent decades, she became a US Senator in 1992.

10 Jerry Brown
Buddhist monk and mayor of Oakland, this intellectual free spirit ran for president.

Left **California Academy of Sciences** Right **Cable Car Museum**

🔟 Museums

1 San Francisco Museum of Modern Art

The city's stylish home for 20th-century European and American art and contemporary multimedia works is a sparkling cultural hub in the South of Market area. Its collections span the whole modern spectrum, from proto-Impressionists to cutting-edge digital installations (see pp26–9).

2 California Academy of Sciences

From 2004–8 the site of this museum at Golden Gate Park is to be renovated and the collection relocated to a temporary home (see pp22–3). This extensive science museum covers virtually every aspect of the natural world.

3 Legion of Honor

This museum, located above Land's End, is one of the city's major venues for pre-modern Western art. It is also a beautiful building in a gorgeous natural setting, so well worth the time it takes to get to. It contains mostly European works, including masterpieces by Rubens, Rembrandt, Georges de la Tour, Degas, Rodin, and Monet. ◎ Lincoln Park, 34th Ave & Clement St • (415) 863-3330 • Map B3 • Open 9:30am–5pm Tue–Sun • Dis. access • Adm • www.thinker.org

The Shades by Auguste Rodin, the Legion of Honor

4 de Young

The old de Young was too damaged in the 1989 earthquake to be saved, but a new state-of-the-art facility opened in 2005. The museum's extensive collection includes a broad range of 19th-century and contemporary American art, as well as pre-Columbian-American, African and Oceanic works. ◎ 50 Hagiwara Tea Garden Drive, Golden Gate Park • Map D4 • (415) 863-3330 • Open 9:30am–5pm Tue–Sun, until 8:45pm Fri • Dis. access • Adm • www.thinker.org

Mexican figure, de Young

5 Asian Art Museum

The new Asian Art Museum is set in the entirely restructured and seismically retrofitted old Main Library in the Civic Center. The vast and important collection of Chinese, Korean, Japanese, Himalayan, and Southeast Asian works is displayed according to their country of origin. But the layout also demonstrates the flow and transformation of Buddhist art from India and outward into the entire Far East. Included is the fabulous Avery Brundage collection of Oriental jade. ◈ *200 Larkin St • Map R2 • (415) 581-3500 • Open 10am–5pm Tue–Sun, 10am–9pm Thur) • Adm • www.asianart.org*

6 Museum of the City of San Francisco

This burgeoning collection traces the city's history, from its low-key Spanish beginnings, to the '49er boom town hoopla, to the modern, complex metropolis it is today. The mementos consist of photos, old newspapers, scale models of buildings, and posters, but one of the most arresting relics is the 3.5-ft (1-m) head of the Goddess of Progress. Her full figure, with electrically illuminated crown, adorned the old City Hall until the 1906 quake toppled her. ◈ *South Light Court, City Hall, Van Ness Ave & Grove St • Map R1 • Open 8am–8pm Mon–Fri, 8am–4pm Sat • Dis. access • Free • www.sfmuseum.org*

7 Cable Car Museum

This brick, warehouse-like structure houses the nuts and bolts machinery that keeps the entire cable car system operating. Don't miss a look downstairs at the giant, spool-like sheaves winding the fat cables round and round *(see p11)*.

8 Musée Mechanique and Holographic Museum

A quaint, time-warp experience awaits you here. As you approach the lower level, you'll be greeted by the loud guffaws of Laughing Sal, the enormous, buxom figure that is a relic of the old Playland at the Beach.

There are also many other often ingenious mechanical devices that once crowded the arcade. Don't miss the re-creation in miniature of a Chinese opium den. In addition, there is a small collection devoted to the art of holography. ◈ *Pier 45, Fisherman's Wharf • Map A3 • Open 11am–7pm Mon–Fri, 10am–8pm Sat–Sun • Free • www.museemechanique.org*

9 Seymour Pioneer Museum

This museum has fascinating historical exhibits of 19th- and 20th-century California. The upstairs gallery displays furniture, sculpture, and paintings. ◈ *300 4th St • Map R5 • (415) 957-1849 • Open 10am–4pm Wed–Sat • Adm • www.california.pioneers.org*

10 Wells Fargo History Museum

The Wells Fargo stagecoaches are the stuff of legends, above all for the tales of their stalwart drivers and the robbers who held them up. Visitors can hear how it must have been to sit on little more than a buckboard for days by listening to the recorded diary of one Francis Brocklehurst. Other exhibits include Pony Express mail, gold nuggets, and photos, and Emperor Norton's currency *(see p54)*. ◈ *420 Montgomery St • Map N5 • Open 9am–5pm Mon–Fri • Free • www.wellsfargohistory.com/museums/*

Bronze stagecoach (1984), Wells Fargo History Museum

Left **Frey Norris Gallery** Right **San Francisco Arts Commission Gallery**

🔟 Art Galleries

1 Fraenkel Gallery

One of the gallery's first exhibitions was of NASA's lunar photographs, and this set a tone for what followed. Soon came exhibitions by Eugene Atget, Edward Weston and Diane Arbus, and later, the Bechers, Adam Fuss, and Sol LeWitt. Projects have brought together work across all media, juxtaposing photography with painting, drawing, and sculpture. Other photographers whose work is regularly shown include Richard Avedon and Man Ray. ◈ 49 Geary St • Map P4 • (415) 981-2661 • Open 10am–5:30pm Tue–Fri, 11am–5pm Sat • Free • www.fraenkelgallery.com

2 Museum of Craft and Folk Art

The emphasis here is on the varieties of non-mainstream ways that people find to be creative – to see things afresh and make something new out of them. This may include traditional folk art from all over the world. ◈ Fort Mason Center, Bldg A • Map F1 • (415) 775-0991 • Open 11am–5pm Tue–Fri & Sun; 10am–5pm Sat • Adm • www.mocfa.org

3 Frey Norris Gallery

This dynamic and extremely stylish contemporary art venue hosts exhibitions of celebrated American and international works, including those by prominent artists from China, Japan, South Korea, and Russia. Bay Area artists are also popular here. The gallery staff provide help and advice to amateur and serious collectors alike about the everchanging contemporary art market. ◈ 456 Geary Street • Map P3 • Open 11am–7pm Tue–Sun • Free

4 Pacific Heritage Museum

Occupying the old San Francisco Mint (1875–7), on top of which the Bank of Canton has been built. The bank sponsors the museum, which focuses on the art of the Pacific Rim, aiming to bring the work of Asian artists to a wider audience. Exhibitions feature many pieces on loan from private collections. ◈ 608 Commercial St • Map N5 • (415) 399-1124 • Open 10am–4pm Tue–Sat • Free • www.ibankunited.com

5 Museo ItaloAmericano

Not only a museum and gallery, but also a community center for San Francisco's Italians. Temporary exhibitions might focus on the work of an Italian artist, or on some aspect of Italian culture. Classes are also offered on Italian art and architecture, and cookery. ◈ Fort Mason Center, Bldg C • Map F1 • Open noon–4pm daily (Mon & Tue by appointment) • Adm

Museum of Craft and Folk Art

6 Galería de la Raza

Bi-monthly exhibitions of Mexican-American art might include painters, cartoonists, performance artists, muralists, or digital installations. Programs also include films, panel discussions, and performances by stars of the Latino art and music scene. ✆ *2857 24th St at Bryant • Map G5 • (415) 826-8009 • Open noon–6pm Wed–Sat • Free • www.galeriadelaraza.org*

7 Intersection for the Arts

Radical and diverse art emerges out of this hotbed of creativity. The alternative multi-genre art installation combines live drama performances, video and film screenings, and panel discussions, which largely explore the influence of race and relationships on people's work and lives. ✆ *446 Valencia St between 15th & 16th sts • Map F4 • (415) 626-2787 • Open noon–5pm Wed–Sat • Free*

8 San Francisco Arts Commission Gallery

Opened in 1970 this was one of the first galleries dedicated to showing the work of emerging Bay Area artists. In addition, the Gallery Slide Registry contains images by more than 500 professional artists from across the US. ✆ *401 Van Ness Ave • Map R1 • (415) 554-6080 • Open noon–5pm Wed–Sat • Free • www.sfagallery.org*

9 SoMarts Gallery

Group and solo shows, music, and readings are a few of the creative goings-on you can encounter here. Founded in 1975, SoMarts is a city-owned cultural center with two exhibition spaces, a 250-seat theater, and printmaking, pottery, and design studios. ✆ *934 Brannan St bet 8th & 9th sts • Map G4 • (415) 863-1414 • Open noon–4pm Tue–Sat • Free*

Cartoon Art Museum

10 Cartoon Art Museum

With an endowment from *Peanuts* creator, the late Charles M. Schulz, the museum is the only one in the US dedicated to cartoon art in all its forms and has approximately 6,000 pieces. ✆ *655 Mission St • Map P5 • (415) CARTOON • Open 11am–5pm Tue–Sun • Adm • www.cartoonart.org*

Left **St. John Coltrane's African Orthodox Church** Right **Cathedral of St. Mary of the Assumption**

Churches

1 Grace Cathedral
San Francisco's own Notre Dame combines Italian Renaissance with a lot of American originality *(see pp24–5)*.

2 Mission Dolores
Photos and a diorama offer a stirring impression of what life was like for the Native Americans who built this Spanish mission in the 18th century *(see pp30–31)*.

3 Cathedral of St. Mary of the Assumption
The exterior of this 1971 building has been compared to a giant washing machine; inside is equally odd, with stained-glass strips, evoking the four elements, and a sculpture of aluminum rods *(see p47)*. ✪ *1111 Gough St • Map F3 • (415) 567-2020 • Services: 6:45am, 8am, 12:10pm Mon–Sat; 7:30am, 9am, 11am Sun • Dis. access • Free*

4 Glide Memorial United Methodist Church
This church has a credo of "the human condition first, not the Bible." Services can draw up to 1,500 celebrants, with a gospel choir and jazz band. This is also one of the religious institutions where same-sex couples can exchange vows of matrimony. ✪ *330 Ellis St • Map Q3 • (415) 674-6000 • Services: 9am & 11am Sun • Free*

5 St. John Coltrane's African Orthodox Church
"My music is the spiritual expression of what I am – my faith, my knowledge, my being." So said famous jazz musician, St. John Coltrane. Services consist of a performance of Coltrane's "A Love Supreme," by the band Ohnedaruth and the Sisters of Compassion choir. ✪ *St Paul's Lutheran Church, 930 Gough St at Turk • Map F3 • Services: 11:45am Sun • Free*

6 First Unitarian Universalist Church
Since 1850, this church has been a progressive voice in the city. Welcoming all faiths and creeds, this congregation is not bound by dogma, but by shared values. ✪ *1187 Franklin St • Map P1 • (415) 776-4580 • Services: 11am Sun • Free • www.uusf.org*

7 St. Mark's Lutheran Church
This 1894 pink-brick church is a mix of Gothic and Romanesque styles. After the 1906 earthquake *(see p37)*, it served as a first-aid station and shelter. ✪ *1111 O'Farrell St • Map P1 • (415) 928-7770 • Services: 9am & 11am Sun • Free • www.sfmarks-sf.org*

Grace Cathedral

Outside of service times, most churches are open to the public free of charge to look around the buildings.

8 St. Patrick's Cathedral
Constructed in 1872, this Gothic Revival cathedral has an impressive marble and stained-glass interior. ◎ 756 Mission St • Map Q4 • (415) 421-3710 • Services: 7am, 8am, 12:10pm, 5:15pm Mon–Sat; 7:30am, 9am, 10:30am, 12:15pm, 5:15pm Sun • Free • www.st-patrick.org

9 Shrine of St. Francis of Assisi
Declared a State Historic Landmark, the Gothic Revival St. Francis of Assisi Church was established on June 17, 1849, as the first parish church in California. The interior is adorned with 11 larger-than-life murals, depicting the works of San Francisco's patron saint. ◎ 610 Vallejo St at Columbus • Map M4 • (415) 983-0405 • Services: 12:15pm Sun–Fri • Free • www.shrinesf.org

10 Sts. Peter & Paul Church
North Beach's landmark "Italian Church" was once dubbed the "Marzipan Church" for the frothy stucco decoration on its soaring pinnacles. Inside, there is a sculpted reproduction of Leonardo da Vinci's *Last Supper* (see p88).

Top 10 Other Places of Worship

1 Kong Chow Temple
The oldest of Chinatown's temples is dedicated to Kuan Di, a male deity *(see pp18–19)*.

2 Tin How Temple
The Queen of Heaven rules this sanctuary and makes sure devotees travel safely by water, among other things *(see pp18–19)*.

3 Temple Sherith Israel
Founded in 1849 by Jewish pioneers, the present domed synagogue dates from 1904. ◎ 2266 California St • Map F3 • Services: 6pm Fri, 10:30am Sat • Free

4 Vedanta Temple
This was the first Hindu Temple (1905) in the western US. ◎ 2963 Webster St • Map E2 • Free

5 Zen Center
Home to the city's Zen practitioners. Beginners are welcome. ◎ 300 Page St • Map F4

6 Crystal Way
Healing through crystals, light, sound, and positive thinking are explored here. ◎ 2335 Market St • Map F5

7 Botanica Yoruba
All the Santeria paraphernalia you'll need *(see p110)*.

8 Psychic Eye Book Shop
A panoply of exotic gods and goddesses. ◎ 301 Fell St • Map F4

9 The Love of Ganesha
Hindu clothing, arts, and crafts. ◎ 1601A Page St • Map E4

10 Open Secret
The backroom of this New Age venue is like a temple to all the world's deities. ◎ 923 C St, San Rafael • Hwy 1

Sts. Peter & Paul Church

Left **San Francisco Museum of Modern Art** Right **Palace of Fine Arts**

Architectural Highlights

1 Transamerica Pyramid
Hated by many at first, the Pyramid is now loved as an icon of the city. Recalling pyramids of ancient cultures, to some it is a symbol of the mysticism that has always played a part in the San Francisco mentality. At 853 ft (260 m), it is the tallest building in the city, but its shape keeps it from casting a shadow on the neighborhood. ✆ 600 Montgomery St • Map N5

2 Bank of America
This 52-story structure was the first skyscraper to be erected in the city, in 1972. The color was a mistake – the granite that faces it was supposed to be pink, not brown, but by the time delivery was made, it was too late. ✆ 555 California St • Map N5

3 San Francisco Museum of Modern Art
Quoting Renaissance architecture in thoroughly modern ways, SFMOMA has established itself as the city's premier Post-Modern effort. The interior has a flexibility and functionality that works perfectly with the collections displayed (see pp26–9).

4 Coit Tower
Perched on Telegraph Hill, this Art Deco sentinel takes the form of a giant fluted column. Reminiscent of Renaissance towers, the column is 63-meters tall and is perforated around the top with arched openings and

windows, which visitors can reach by elevator for stunning views of the city (see p88).

5 Palace of Fine Arts
This bit of Neo-Classical fluff was designed by Bernard Maybeck for the Pan-Pacific Exposition of 1915. It is patterned on an 18th-century engraving by Giovanni Piranesi entitled The Isle of the Dead (see p94).

6 Civic Center
Centered on the City Hall that would do any state proud, the core buildings are in a grand Beaux-Arts style; and befitting the city that started the Gold Rush, gilt is everywhere (see p84).

7 Haas-Lilienthal House
This Queen Anne-style mansion, built in 1886, is one of the few Victorian beauties in the city that accepts callers. It's a wonderful glimpse into the way of life among San Francisco's upper-middle classes from about 1890 to 1920. Outside, it features

Haas-Lilienthal House

For a walking tour of the city's famous Victorian houses, contact (415) 252-9485 or visit www.victorianwalk.com

Transamerica Pyramid

gables, a turret, and patterned embellishments; inside, you can see parlors, a dining room, one of six bedrooms, and the ball-room, all with period furniture. Ⓢ *2007 Franklin St • Map M1 • Open noon–3pm Wed, 11am–4pm Sun • Adm*

8 Grace Cathedral
Executed in the medieval French Gothic style, echoing in particular Notre Dame in Paris, yet accomplished using steel-reinforced concrete. It is the third largest Episcopal church in the US *(see pp24–5)*.

9 Folk Art International
Dating from 1948, this is the city's only building by Frank Lloyd Wright. The sweeping spiral ramp predates that at Wright's Guggenheim Museum in New York. Ⓢ *140 Maiden Lane • Map P4 • (415) 392-9999 • Open 10am–6pm Mon–Sat • Free • www.folkartintl.com*

10 St. Mary's Cathedral
Critics abound who are ready to dismiss this parabolic form, but the soaring curves take the attention upward, in much the same fashion that tracery and peaked vaulting do in Gothic cathedrals *(see p44)*.

Top 10 Public Art Sites

1 Balmy Alley
The most famous set of murals in town, by local Latino artists. Ⓢ *24th & 25th sts between Harrison and Treat • Map G6*

2 San Francisco Art Institute
Diego Rivera, the Mexican muralist, painted *The Making of a Fresco* here. Ⓢ *800 Chestnut St • Map K3*

3 Coit Tower
Depression-era murals decorate the lobby *(see p88)*.

4 Fort Mason
The Learning Wall is a mural depicting education. Ⓢ *Franklin St • Map J1*

5 Women's Building
The work of seven women painters graces the façade. Ⓢ *18th St between Valencia & Guerrero • Map F5*

6 Bikeway
This 340-ft (104-m) mural chronicles a bike-ride from Downtown to Ocean Beach. Ⓢ *Duboce St between Church & Market • Map F4*

7 Beach Chalet
Depression-era murals depict famous citizens. Ⓢ *1000 Great Hwy • Map A4*

8 Rincon Center
These 1948 murals by Russian artist Anton Refregier trace Californian history. Ⓢ *Mission, Howard, Steuart & Spear sts • Map H2*

9 Financial District
The black-stone *Transcendence* is in front of the Bank of America.

10 Golden Gate Park
The Music Concourse is adorned with a number of bronzes, including *Apple Cider Press (see pp20–21)*.

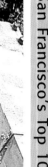

There are walking and biking tours showcasing murals in the Mission District. Contact (415) 285-2287 for details.

Left **Embarcadero Park** Right **Buena Vista Park**

TOP 10 **Parks and Gardens**

1 Golden Gate Park
One of the largest city parks in the US is also one of the most diverse, and all of it brought forth from what was once scrub and dunes. The park also features first-rate cultural attractions such as the California Academy of Sciences *(see pp20–23)*.

2 Buena Vista Park
This steep and densely wooded hill offers terrific panoramas from its Haight Street location, as well as some fairly challenging trails for those who like to hike and bike. ✪ *Map E4*

3 Fort Mason
The rolling lawn above Fort Mason Center *(see p94)*, known as the Great Meadow, is a relatively little-used park, but it's great for taking a siesta, tossing a frisbee, or just strolling through to take in the spectacular views from the cliffs. ✪ *Map F1*

Shakespeare Garden, Golden Gate Park

4 The Presidio
This vast swathe of greenery has only recently entered the city's repertoire of parklands. It has the potential to be even more amazing than Golden Gate Park, providing that the right decisions are made by the Presidio Trust, whose job it is to make the new national park financially self-sufficient by 2013. The war of words and proposals is raging at the moment, mostly over exactly how commercialized the property should be allowed to become *(see p95)*.

5 Alta Plaza
Pacific Heights's double block of verdant hill is a popular place to take the sun when it ventures to break through the fog. Basketball and tennis courts and a children's playground are in the center, while to the south there are terraced lawns, onto which some of Pacific Heights' oldest homes face. ✪ *Map E2*

6 Alamo Square
Postcard central, thanks to its row of perfect Victorians backed by the knock-out Downtown view. The park itself is a sloping patch of green, while the surrounding streets are lined with so many grand old houses that it has been declared a historic site. Two of them have been turned into hotels, although the areas immediately outside the square are not the most salubrious at night. ✪ *Map E4*

Note: San Francisco's parks should be avoided at night.

7 Embarcadero Park

The last few years have witnessed a welcome transformation along the entire stretch of the Embarcadero. The 1989 earthquake put an end to the idea of running a freeway into the city center, so the old shipping piers are now set off by new plantings and sidewalks and the area is being promoted as a breezy park. In-line skaters and cyclists disport themselves where once concrete embankments held sway (see p93).

8 Yerba Buena Gardens

A small but very welcome patch of green in an otherwise paved-over area. When the weather is fine, the lawn is populated by sunbathers, while other parts of the gardens feature beautiful memorial fountains and sculptures (see p28).

9 Lafayette Park

This is another of Pacific Heights's double-blocked hilltop gardens – a leafy green haven of pine and eucalyptus. Steep stairways lead to the summit, with its delightful views. The city did not manage to set aside

Lafayette Park

these oases without a fight. Squatters' buildings occupied some of the land in the center of this park until as late as 1936, when they were finally pulled down, liberating the lush gardens for all to enjoy. ◈ Map F2

10 Walton Park

This tiny park is a much needed break from concrete and asphalt for Downtown workers, whom you will see picnicking here at weekday lunchtimes. The park evokes a peaceful mountain meadow. A wonderful sculpture by Georgia O'Keeffe adds contrast, while a central fountain sends droplets of water falling across cement blocks below. ◈ Map M6

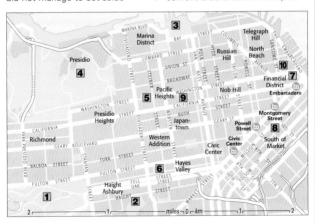

Left **Gumps** Right **Embarcadero Center**

🔟 Stores and Shopping Centers

1 Gumps
Founded in 1861 by German immigrants, this homegrown department store is an institution. It has the largest collection in the US of fine china and crystal, selling famous names such as Baccarat and Lalique. The store is also celebrated for its Oriental treasures, rare works of art, and its window displays. ◈ *135 Post St • Map P4 • (800) 766-7628*

2 Nordstrom
Located on the top five floors of this gleaming center, the fashion emporium is known as the "store in the sky." Impeccable service, a vast selection, and a refined atmosphere featuring live piano music make this a very upscale shopping experience. ◈ *San Francisco Shopping Center, 865 Market St • Map Q4*

3 Neiman Marcus
Perhaps the highest of the high-end stores, this one overlooks Union Square from a plum spot once occupied by the City

Nordstrom

of Paris building, constructed in the 1890s but torn down to build this modern structure. Part of the original remains, however, by way of the huge stained-glass dome. Neiman's boast is that it can get anything you might want – private jets, elephants, you name it. ◈ *150 Stockton St • Map P4*

4 Saks Fifth Avenue
For decades, the name has been synonymous with high style and this branch of the New York mainstay is one of the best embodiments of the store's mythic elan. You'll find just about every international designer of note here. ◈ *384 Post St • Map P4*

5 Macy's
This old-guard department store has now become an all-purpose emporium carrying merchandise in all price ranges. Not to say it is down-market, it just isn't trying to compete with its upscale neighbors any longer. ◈ *170 O'Farrell St • Map P4*

6 Crocker Galleria
In the 1980s, when an old office building was truncated, architects put together some of the vintage elements to create this sparkling indoor mall. Its three floors are under a dramatic glass dome built around a central plaza, creating an open-ended arcade. US and European designer stores vie for attention with local shops, cafés, and restaurants. ◈ *50 Post St • Map P5*

For tips on shopping in San Francisco See p140

Crocker Galleria

7 Embarcadero Center

These four skyscrapers are primarily office towers, but on the lower and promenade levels there are over 125 shops and restaurants, from newsstands and coffee bars to a Gap. The choice tends toward the major chains. ◎ *Embarcadero & Battery, Sacramento & Clay sts • Map N6*

8 Ghirardelli Square

Housing over 70 restaurants and shops, this former chocolate factory has become one of the most frequented destinations in Fisherman's Wharf. The stores range from tourist T-shirt shops to fine jewelry boutiques *(see p13)*. ◎ *900 North Point St • Map K1*

9 Metreon

This showcase for Sony products and similar paraphernalia is a high-tech heaven for kids *(see p59)*. ◎ *101 4th St • Map Q4*

10 San Francisco Shopping Center

The crown of San Francisco's main shopping mall is Nordstrom, but there are some 100 shops and boutiques spread over its nine floors. ◎ *865 Market St • Map Q4*

Top 10 Shopping Areas

1 Union Square
Traditionally the focal point of all the best stores, including Tiffany & Co, Armani, Prada, Cartier, Yves St Laurent, Chanel, and more *(see p84)*.

2 Union Street
Converted Victorian homes house a charming assortment of boutiques, bookstores, antiques shops, restaurants, and a cinema *(see p99)*.

3 Grant Avenue
The southernmost four blocks are chic shopping off Union Square; then you enter eight blocks of exotic Chinatown emporiums; finally, Upper Grant is all about North Beach hangouts. ◎ *Map N4*

4 Upper Fillmore Street
A colorful choice of cafés, restaurants, and boutiques, all geared to a high-end Pacific Heights clientele. ◎ *Map E2*

5 Market Street
A good place to find cut-rate electronics shops, as well as outlet shops like Old Navy clothing store. ◎ *Map Q3*

6 Hayes Valley
These blocks offer shopping with an avant garde feel *(see p100)*.

7 Chestnut Street
Clothing boutiques, health-food shops, and an old-fashioned cinema. ◎ *Map K1*

8 The Mission
Plenty of super-discount stores and funky home furnishing shops *(see p108)*.

9 Castro Street
Fine shops, gay bookstores and erotic boutiques *(see p107)*.

10 Haight Street
This is still hippie-central – secondhand clothing and esoteric emporiums *(see p99)*.

Left **Jack London** Right **Dashiell Hammett**

🔟 Writers

1 Jack London

Adventurer and author of frontier tales such as *White Fang*, *The Sea Wolf*, and *The Call of the Wild*, Jack London (1876–1916) grew up in Oakland. There a museum of his memorabilia is housed in a reconstruction of the log cabin he lived in while prospecting for gold in the Yukon Territory. His fiction is based on his experiences in the untamed West and the social inequality he saw in boom town San Francisco.

2 Dashiell Hammett

The author of *The Maltese Falcon* and creator of the classic hard-boiled detective Sam Spade made San Francisco his home from 1921 to 1929. He used the fog-swirled slopes of the city's hills as the perfect backdrop for his stylish crime stories. Hammett (1884–1961) was himself employed briefly at the famous Pinkerton Detective Agency.

3 Gertrude Stein & Alice B. Toklas

Stein (1874–1946) was raised in Oakland, Toklas (1877–1967) in San Francisco, and both were members of the wealthy Jewish bourgeoisie that has played such an important part in the city's cultural life. But these two larger-than-life women soon deserted the Bay Area for Paris, where they became Queen Bees of a circle of brilliant international artists and writers, including Pablo Picasso and Ernest Hemingway.

4 Jack Kerouac

Arriving from New York in 1947, it was Kerouac (1922–69) who coined the term "Beat." He and his companions – Neal Cassady, Allen Ginsberg, Lawrence Ferlinghetti, and others – initiated the new politics of dissent and free love, all of which led, within a decade, to the Hippie Movement *(see p37)*. His classic novel *On the Road* (1957) galvanized a generation.

5 Allen Ginsberg

Ginsberg (1926–97) cleared the way for the eventual Gay Liberation Movement by openly declaring his homosexuality in his literary milestone *Howl*, first unveiled to the public in 1955 *(see p37)*. His epic poem soon attracted charges of obscenity in the buttoned-down, witch-hunting 1950s. Ginsberg's spiritual mysticism also set the tone for the Hippie Movement.

Jack Kerouac

Armistead Maupin

Top 10 Movies Set in San Francisco

1 San Francisco
Clark Gable and Jeannette Macdonald star in this 1936 film set amid the rubble of the 1906 earthquake.

2 The Maltese Falcon
Classic Bogart (1941), in which he embodies detective Sam Spade. The four-year-old Bay Bridge is in evidence.

3 Dark Passage
This Humphrey Bogart and Lauren Bacall vehicle (1947) makes use of San Francisco's moody climate.

4 Vertigo
A classic Alfred Hitchcock thriller (1958) memorably shows the crashing waves under Golden Gate Bridge.

5 Bullitt
Probably the most famous car-chase ever filmed, due to the city's infamous hills (1968).

6 Dirty Harry
Yet another detective story (1971) set in the city that invites such mysteries, perhaps due to its fog.

7 Invasion of the Body Snatchers
This 1978 remake of the 1950s classic stars Donald Sutherland as the last survivor of a chilling alien takeover.

8 The Woman in Red
Famous sights play important roles in this 1984 comedy starring Gene Wilder.

9 Basic Instinct
This 1992 thriller sees Sharon Stone and Michael Douglas cross Golden Gate Bridge to a love-pad at Seadrift.

10 Mrs Doubtfire
Native San Franciscan Robin Williams is in drag in this 1993 spoof. Golden Gate Park is shown to full effect.

6 Armistead Maupin
Maupin's *Tales of the City* were serialized in the *San Francisco Chronicle* before being published in book form. They are lighthearted paeans to the idiosyncrasies of gay San Francisco in the 1970s, before the specter of AIDS changed everything.

7 Alice Walker
African-American feminist and dedicated San Franciscan, Walker's novel *The Color Purple* (1985) set the tone for a new vision of black heritage, as seen from the woman's point of view.

8 Wallace Stegner
A Stanford professor of creative writing, Stegner's novel *Angle of Repose* won the Pulitzer Prize in 1972.

9 Amy Tan
When Tan's *The Joy Luck Club* (1989) hit the scene, San Francisco's Chinese community at last found its voice. It illustrated Chinese culture and its clash with uprooted Americana.

10 Danielle Steele
Steele's "bodice-rippers" have had such success that she can now afford to be mistress of the very finest Pacific Heights mansion *(see p99)*.

One of Wallace Stegner's most famous students was Ken Kesey, author of the bestseller One Flew Over the Cuckoo's Nest.

San Francisco's Top 10

Left **Joshua Abraham Norton** Center **Joan Baez** Right **Willie Brown**

TOP 10 Eccentric & Noteworthy Characters

1 Sally Sanford
The Sausalito Chart House Restaurant is the former purview of Sally Sanford (1903–82), the one-time bawdy house doyenne, and then Honorary Mayor of Sausalito. Since Gold Rush days, San Francisco has loved and even honored those who stand for the city's sexual liberality.

2 Joshua Abraham Norton
Born in 1819, Norton made his fortune in San Francisco but lost it all in 1852. The event left him unhinged but harmless, and he declared himself "Emperor of the United States and Protector of Mexico." He issued his own money, and was lovingly indulged by the city's populace until his death in 1880.

3 Jello Biafra
Punk rock lead vocalist for The Dead Kennedys, Biafra ran for mayor of San Francisco in 1979. His basic belief was that corrupt governments and corporations should be fought, not trusted. He chose the name Jello Biafra because of "the way the two images collide in people's minds," with "Jello" as the embodiment of American blandness and "Biafra" as the universal symbol of starvation. His platform included having businessmen wear clown suits to the office. He finished fourth out of a field of ten, with 3.5 per cent of the total votes.

4 Sister Boom-Boom
One of the original Sisters of Perpetual Indulgence, a self-described order of gay male nuns, Sister Boom-Boom took part in street theater with them in the late 1970s and early 1980s. In 1982 he ran for a seat on the Board of Supervisors of San Francisco, winning 23,125 votes. He is also a recognized astrologer and uses New Age science to interpret gay issues for the community.

5 Melvin Belli
Known as the "King of Torts", the flamboyant Belli was a pivotal figure in fostering today's litigious society as an innovator in the area of personal injury law. He took on big corporations and controversial clients, including Errol Flynn, Jim and Tammy Faye Bakker, Lana Turner, Mae West, Muhammad Ali, and Jack Ruby. Belli died in 1996 at the age of 88, just a few months after filing for bankruptcy.

Jello Biafra and The Dead Kennedys

6 Joan Baez
Known in her youth as "The Voice," girlfriend of Bob Dylan, and peacenik, the Palo Alto native later came out as a lesbian, continuing to work for peace and social justice. Recently, Baez created a cabaret character, the Contessa ZinZanni, in a show that has enjoyed good reviews in San Francisco.

7 Mrs. Madrigal
Olympia Dukakis brought this wonderful *Tales of the City* character to vibrant life in the mini-series based on Armistead Maupin's books *(see p53)*. Anna Madrigal is a transsexual landlady who rents out apartments to young singles, both gay and straight, and tends to her marijuana plants and her charges with equal wisdom and spirituality.

8 Francis Ford Coppola
Another native son, the director of *The Godfather* makes San Francisco the home of his Zoetrope productions, and has also branched out into other enterprises. His Niebaum-Coppola winery in the Napa Valley is one of the best.

9 Herb Caen
For nearly six decades Caen's newspaper column was required reading. To his many devoted fans he was, and remains "Mr. San Francisco." He coined the term "Beatnik" in his April 2, 1958, column.

10 Willie Brown
San Francisco's first African-American mayor is famous for his *bon vivant* ways. His high-living, fast-shuffling style has not detracted from his popularity, however, and the city seems to have prospered under his tutelage.

Top 10 Sixties Figures

1 Janis Joplin
This troubled singer from Texas became the queen of the San Francisco sound, until her death by heroin overdose.

2 Ken Kesey
A powerful, revolutionary writer, his Magic Bus and Trips Festival set the tone for the entire Hippie Movement.

3 Jerry Garcia
Patriarch of the San Francisco sound, his Grateful Dead band continued to tour until his death in 1995.

4 Mario Savio
The UC Berkeley student launched the Free Speech Movement on the campus in the late 1960s.

5 Owsley Stanley
The most famous source of pure LSD in the 1960s.

6 Grace Slick
The other queen of San Francisco's influential bands, in this case Jefferson Airplane.

7 Huey Newton
Oakland's founder of the Black Panthers, a group committed to violent change if necessary.

8 Patty Hearst
The newspaper heiress, kidnapped by the Symbionese Liberation Army in 1974, apparently converted and took part in an armed robbery.

9 Jim Jones
The leader of a Fillmore District religious group who moved en masse to South America ended his days and those of some 900 followers in 1978, in a mass suicide by cyanide-laced Kool-Aid.

10 Charles Manson
This commune leader and his followers murdered actress Sharon Tate in 1969.

Left **Louise M. Davies Symphony Hall** Right **War Memorial Opera House**

TOP10 **Performing Arts Venues**

1 War Memorial Opera House and San Francisco Ballet

The San Francisco Opera Company is the second largest in the country and performs from June to January. The excellent San Francisco Ballet, one of the nation's oldest, mostly performs at the Opera House, too *(see p84)*. ❀ *301 Van Ness Ave • Map R1 • (415) 864-3330*

2 Louise M. Davies Symphony Hall

With performances from September to May, under the directorship of Michael Tilson Thomas, the San Francisco Symphony Orchestra performs in this modern structure with carefully modulated acoustics. Built in 1980, this curving, glass-fronted concert hall is loved and loathed in equal measure by San Franciscans. Its corner placement is set off by a Henry Moore bronze, which also has its share of detractors. ❀ *201 Van Ness Ave • Map R1 • (415) 864-6000*

San Francisco Symphony Orchestra

3 Masonic Auditorium

Originally a Masonic Temple, built in 1957, this attractive structure, with its 3,000-seat auditorium, is used as a venue for jazz performances, lectures, and readings, as well as conventions and seminars. Mosaics inside and out depict some of the tenets of Freemasonry. ❀ *1111 California St • Map N3 • (415) 776-4702*

4 Curran Theater

Built in 1922, this is one of the grandest theaters in the city and a Registered National Historic Landmark. The interior is a fantasy of gold and carved wood, complemented by a vast chandelier and murals. Shows tend toward long-running Broadway hits. ❀ *445 Geary St • Map P3 • (415) 551-2000 • www.shnsf.com*

5 Golden Gate Theater

This former movie house, designed with Moorish influences in the 1920s, is one of the larger mainstream theaters. Its usual offerings are traveling Broadway shows – most recently, hits imported from New York have included a revival of *Damn Yankees*, starring Jerry Lewis. ❀ *1 Taylor St • Map Q3 • (415) 551-2000 • www.shnsf.com*

6 Herbst Theater

The smallest of the mainstream houses offers a mix of cabaret, comedy, dance, lectures, and concerts. It's really just a recital hall, and the acoustics are

If you want to see some of the most popular shows in San Francisco, it is always wise to book well in advance.

Orpheum

not great, but the beautiful 1930s building is decorated with eight enormous Beaux-Arts murals that were executed for the 1915 Pan-Pacific Exposition. ✧ *Veterans' Memorial Building, 401 Van Ness Ave • Map Q1 • (415) 392-4400*

7 Orpheum

Originally a vaudeville house and then a movie theater, this is the historic spot where *Hair* was given its first West Coast performance some three decades ago – known locally as "the New York version of what happened here in San Francisco." The theater, decorated in 1920s Moorish taste, now mostly stages Broadway shows. ✧ *1192 Market St • Map R2 • (415) 551-2000 • www.shnsf.com*

8 American Conservatory Theater (ACT)

Founded in the 1960s, San Francisco's most important theater company is internationally respected and has produced premieres of a number of major plays. At the heart of ACT is one of the most acclaimed actor-training institutions in the nation – former students include Denzel Washington, Annette Bening, and Winona Ryder. ✧ *Geary Theater, 415 Geary St • Map P3 • (415) 749-2228*

9 Magic Theater

In the 1970s, none other than Sam Shepard was the resident playwright of the Magic, and its stage has seen performances by the likes of Sean Penn and Nick Nolte. It specializes in bringing new plays to light, usually by up-and-coming Americans. It also offers "raw play" readings of as yet unstaged works. ✧ *Fort Mason Center, Bldg D • Map F1 • (415) 441-8822*

10 Beach Blanket Babylon

High camp and high head-dresses, along with jolly good singing by the veteran ensemble cast make this one of the joys of the city. It's been zinging the heartstrings of lovers of San Francisco for more than a quarter of a century and shows no signs of flagging. The excuse for all this frivolity is the sending up of various notables, most of whom well deserve the good-natured ribbing. ✧ *Club Fugazi, 678 Green St • Map L4 • (415) 421-4222*

Left **Golden Gate Park playground** Right **Exploratorium**

🔟 Children's Attractions

1 Exploratorium
Kids can experience one of the finest, uniquely San Francisco interactive days at this superb science museum. They'll learn all about their senses and how they work, as well as delve into all the laws of physics through first-hand experiments. The top draw, however, is the Tactile Dome, a totally dark sphere in which you feel your way along, touching a range of sensorially stimulating objects and textures (see p94).

Crazy Castle, San Francisco Zoo

2 San Francisco Zoo
Direct encounters with farm animals at Family Farm, and visits with zoo babies, which may include gorillas, snow leopards, rhinos, or alpacas, make this a must-do for the youngsters. Although perhaps not the biggest or best zoo in the world, its attention to top-quality children's programs, such as the many feeding times and the creepy-crawly insect denizens, make it one of the tops for budding zoologists. The whole landscaping of the place, from quirky castles to natural habitats, is also designed for maximum fun (see p116).

3 Aquariums
Part of Golden Gate Park's California Academy of Sciences (see pp22–3), the Steinhart Aquarium is a big hit with kids. The darkened corridors are filled with softly glowing tanks in which some of the weirdest creatures on the planet disport themselves. Then there's the Touching Tidal Pool if kids want to get up close and personal with their finny friends. At Fisherman's Wharf, UnderWater World gives an even greater undersea experience, with walk-through transparent tunnels surrounded by sea life (see p13).

4 Zeum
This elaborate complex, aimed both at entertaining kids and spurring their creativity to the max, is part of the greater Yerba Buena Center. There's a wonderful old-fashioned carousel, a labyrinth, a studio where they can script, produce, and star in their own videos, art studios and galleries, plus lots more to keep them busy and productive all day long. Ages 5 to 18 (see p28).

Alcatraz

5 Randall Museum

Perched above the city, in Corona Heights Park, this small, welcoming complex is primarily a petting zoo, with farm animals, raccoons, reptiles, and birds. But it also offers hands-on experience with woodworking, pottery, painting, theater, photography, model railroads, storytelling, gardening, and more. The aim is to teach children respect for nature and the environment.
🛈 199 Museum Way, off Roosevelt Way, Buena Vista • Map E4 • (415) 554-9600 • Open 10am–5pm Tue–Sat • Free • www.randallmuseum.org

6 Alcatraz

"The Rock" is always a hit with older children, particularly boys, who relate immediately to the grim, quasi-military aspects of the place. The wildness of the island's natural beauty, as well as the great ferry ride out and back, will also delight. Smaller kids might find the place a bit frightening (see pp14–17).

7 Bay Area Discovery Museum

This hands-on museum is aimed directly at children. Kids will be able to enjoy an underwater sea tunnel, an art studio, a science lab, an engineering lab, the "Maze of Illusions," and a media center. 🛈 557 McReynolds Rd, Sausalito • (415) 339-3900 • Open 9am–4pm Tue–Fri, 10am–5pm Sat–Sun • Dis. access • Adm • www.baykidsmuseum.org

8 Golden Gate Park Playground

At the southeastern corner of the park, kids will love the old carousel, a treehouse, and some great swings, slides, and other kid-driven rides. In the summer, there are often Punch and Judy shows to tickle and delight children of all ages (see pp20–23).

9 Angel Island State Park

An ideal place for a full-day family outing. You can picnic, swim, hike, kayak, camp, or take the tram tour that goes all around the island, with a guide who points out sites of historic interest – dating from the days when the place was a rather forbidding immigrant clearing station (see p93).

10 Metreon

Intended as a lively, high-tech, multilevel amusement arcade for adolescents, so far the only thing that seems to have clicked is the superb cinema complex. Here you can see the latest Hollywood blockbusters with full digital sound effects amped up to the highest possible level. Otherwise, the Metreon's darkened rooms, designed for checking out the latest video games, are largely abandoned by the teens who were supposed to be flocking (see p29).

Angel Island State Park

Left **Divisadero** Right **Twin Peaks**

🔟 Scenic Drives

1 49-Mile Drive

This all-in-one driving tour is marked with blue-and-white seagull markers, and winds its way through the most picturesque parts of the city. It can be challenging to follow, keeping an eye out for the markers and the traffic at the same time, but you can get a map of the route from the Visitor Information Center *(see p132)*.

49-Mile Drive marker

2 Mount Tamalpais

The road that leads up to the top of "Mount Tam" is appropriately called Panoramic Highway. All the way along, it provides you with dramatic views of the Marin Headlands, both on the Bay and ocean sides, and as you approach the summit, far-reaching views of the Bay Area *(see p124)*.

3 Conzelman Road

This road hugs the bluffs, high above the waves, on the southern edge of the Marin Headlands. It affords some of the most famously beautiful views of the north tower of Golden Gate Bridge, looking back at the city in the distance. The way is punctuated with old military bunkers, since this entire area was once given over to the army to guard the western shores. ◈ *Marin County*

4 Twin Peaks

More famous panoramas await you here, as you wind your way up the two mountains. You can get 360-degree views of the city to the east, the ocean to the west, the Bay to the north, and the valleys to the south *(see p107)*.

5 The Great Highway

Broad and straight, this coast highway begins at Cliff House at the northern end and eventually meets the famous Highway 1, which takes you, via dramatic cliffs, down to Half Moon Bay, Santa Cruz, Monterey, Carmel, Big Sur – and eventually, to Mexico. ◈ *Map A4*

6 Divisadero

This street cuts a great swathe through the city centre. It starts in the south at Duboce Street, then rises to glorious mansions and Bay vistas after Geary Expressway. ◈ *Map E4*

7 Berkeley & Oakland Hills

Blending gently with the Berkeley Hills, the Oakland Hills offer some beautiful parks, such as Redwood Regional Park. Skyline Boulevard provides access to most of this ridge area, with many picnic groves and hiking options along the winding way. ◈ *Hwy 24*

8 Skyline Drive
Pick up this bucolic road (Highway 35) at Lake Merced *(see p117)*, and it will take you all the way down the woody spine of the Peninsula to Santa Cruz. It's a total immersion in nature, just minutes from the populated areas around the Bay.

9 La Honda & Old La Honda Roads
Behind Stanford University *(see p125)* is the quiet town of Portola Valley. From here, these picturesque switchback roads ascend to meet Skyline Drive. They are very narrow in places, and you can't go more than 10 mph (16 kmph), but the timeless beauty of the Bay Area forests makes it worthwhile.

10 Highway 9 and Big Basin State Park
This gently mountainous region is almost entirely undeveloped. The main town, Boulder Creek, is like a small frontier settlement, where craftspeople sell their wares, and country stores cater mostly to locals. This is an area that time happily forgot.

Highway 1, from The Great Highway

Top 10 Hair-Raising Hills

1 Lombard Street
Called "The Crookedest Street in the World," it isn't too hair-raising, but the views of North Beach as you descend are charming. Map L1

2 Top of Divisadero
The most dramatic section of Divisadero is the highest point in Pacific Heights. Map E2

3 Twin Peaks
The view from these peaks seems like one from a helicopter, hovering over the city. Map E6

4 Gough between Jackson and Washington
A hair-raising ascent, especially if your car isn't automatic – it's *very* steep. Map F2

5 Sacramento up Nob Hill
Take the bus up and hear the engine churning on its painfully slow ascent. Map N3

6 Noe at 21st Street
At the heights bordering the Castro, Noe Valley, and the Mission, this impossibly steep street will also give you a few chills. Map F5

7 Potrero Hill
Try Wisconsin Street at 20th for an experience that feels like freefall *(see p109)*.

8 Corona Heights Park
Hiking trails and some spectacular views. Map E4

9 Russian Hill
One of the best drives in town, with great views of Fisherman's Wharf. Map M2

10 Filbert Street
There's a sense of flying off into space as you dive over the brink of Hyde and Leavenworth. Map L2

Left **Rubicon** Right **Ritz-Carlton Hotel Dining Room**

🔟 Restaurants

1 The Ritz-Carlton Hotel Dining Room

More perfect food than this, in a more quietly refined setting, or with more elegantly considerate service is hard to imagine. When you want to give yourself a treat, make a reservation here and prepare to be pampered with the very best food and wines *(see p91)*.

2 Kokkari Estiatorio

This upscale Greek taverna is a fun and spirited place that might have you imagining yourself to be somewhere in the Aegean. Don't bypass the appetizer sample, which includes homemade pitta bread, and various artfully delicious spreads. ⊗ *200 Jackson St at Front • Map M6 • (415) 981-0983 • Dis. access • $$$*

3 Rubicon

Great California-French fusion cooking that is always delicious and never fails to wow the devoted clientele of this Financial District high-power dining experience. Excellent wine list, beautiful presentation, and superior service *(see p91)*.

4 Taqueria Cancun

With its much-deserved cult following, this is the locals' first choice for cheap, satisfying, and fast Mex fare. Its secret? A red-hot salsa and tortillas that are grilled (not steamed). ⊗ *2288 Mission St at 19th • Map F5 • (415) 252-9560 • No credit cards • Dis. access • $*

5 Greens

Originally inspired by the huge success of the Zen bakery and coffee shop, this spacious, pleasant Marina restaurant soon came to define vegetarian eating – substantial, delicious, and inventive – for the entire Bay Area *(see p97)*.

6 Delfina

Nouvelle Italian might best describe the cuisine here, and it is turned out to near perfection. The decor is fairly stark but not overbearing, and the inventive dishes rarely fail to surprise and delight. Maybe you'll choose a night when they're serving gnocchi with peas and morel mushrooms. ⊗ *3621 18th St between Dolores and Guerrero • Map F5 • (415) 552-4055 • Closed L • Dis. access • $$*

Delfina

LuLu
7 The setting is modeled on Michelangelo's Piazza del Campidoglio, and the large oak-burning rotisseries and ovens complete the Roman theme. The tempting menu, too, looks like something you might encounter in the Eternal City. ◈ *816 Folsom St • Map R5 • (415) 495-5775 • Dis. access • $$$*

Ahi Tuna

Aqua
8 Aqua specializes in fish and the must-have is the tartare of ahi tuna. Gorgeous decor and presentation. ◈ *252 California St • Map N6 • (415) 956-9662 • Closed Sat & Sun L • Dis. access • $$$$$*

Foreign Cinema
9 In the courtyard, old movies are projected onto a neighboring building while you dine. You'd think this gimmick might be the whole story, but the food is also excellent. The oyster bar and Sunday brunch on the patio are popular. ◈ *2534 Mission St • Map F5 • (415) 648-7600 • Dis. access • $$*

Royal Thai
10 One of the best Thai restaurants around. You can't beat it for freshness and flavor – but it's very, very spicy. ◈ *610 3rd St at Irwin, San Rafael • Hwy 101 • (415) 485-1074 • Dis. access • $$*

Top 10 Romantic Dinner Spots

Garden Court
1 The stained-glass ceiling and marble columns make this one of the most sumptuous restaurants. ◈ *Sheraton Palace Hotel, 2 New Montgomery St • Map P5 • (415) 546-5089 • Dis. access • $$$*

Cliff House
2 A wild coastal setting, with views of crashing waves (see p115).

Acquerello
3 The black truffles are said to be an aphrodisiac. ◈ *1722 Sacramento St • Map N1 • (415) 567-5432 • $$$$*

Masa's Hotel Vintage Court
4 French Mediterranean cuisine in elegant surroundings. ◈ *648 Bush St • Map 4N • (415) 989-7154 • $$$$*

Boulevard
5 *Belle époque* decor and extravagant food (see p113).

Caffè Centro
6 Popular with 20-something couples (see p113)

Chenery Park
7 Take a window seat looking out onto the street for the maximum effect. ◈ *683 Chenery St • Map F6 • (415) 337-8537 • Dis. access • $$*

Alta Mira
8 Some of the best views on the Bay. ◈ *125 Bulkley St, Sausalito • Hwy 101 • (415) 332-1350 • $$*

Lark Creek Inn
9 One of the loveliest garden settings on the Bay (see p129).

Chez Panisse
10 The birthplace of Cal-Med cuisine. Book weeks ahead. ◈ *1517 Shattuck Ave, Berkeley • Hwy 80 • (510) 548-5525 • Dis. access • $$$$*

Left **Caffè Trieste** Right **Café Flore**

Top 10 Cafés

1 Café Claude
The owner actually bought Le Barbizon Café in Paris and shipped it over piece by piece. That accounts for the authentic French feel of this back-alley bistro-like spot near Union Square, where francophiles rendezvous to imagine themselves on the Left Bank. The food, too, is suitably Gallic. ◎ *7 Claude Lane between Grant & Kearny, Sutter & Bush • Map P4 • (415) 392-3505 • Dis. access*

2 Caffè Trieste
A North Beach landmark that must be experienced if you have any interest whatsoever in this quarter's colorful history – either from the literary and artistic or the Italian points of view. It's a really great place for a cup of whatever warm liquid you favor, and to just sit and people-watch or dip into one of the city's free weekly papers *(see p90)*.

Café Claude

3 Steps of Rome
One of the many Italian cafés – often full of real Italians - lined up along this stretch of Columbus. This one features large windows, usually open, with clientele spilling out onto the sidewalk to eye the stream of passers-by. Good coffee and desserts make it an appealing pit stop until closing time at 2am. ◎ *348 Columbus Ave between Broadway & Vallejo • Map M4 • (415) 397-0435*

4 South Park Café
Overlooking the small SoMa park favored by the younger, slacker digital set, you can while away an hour or two just taking in the relaxed setting in the knowledge that you're in a certifiably hip locale. French food and waiters support the Parisian illusion to the best of their ability. ◎ *108 South Park St between 2nd & 3rd • Map H3 • (415) 495-7275 • Dis. access*

5 Brainwash
Café, bar, performance space, and, yes, laundromat, it's got everything the young apartment dwellers who live in this industrial SoMa neighborhood need. Frequented by lesbians, gays, and straights – in short, typical San Franciscans of the edgier sort. There's also a menu composed of solid international standards, such as a great Greek salad, tofu stir-fry, and chicken quesadilla. ◎ *1122 Folsom St at 7th • Map R3 • (415) 861-3663 • Dis. access*

Brainwash

6 Atlas Café
This enclave features live acoustic music on Thursday night and Saturday afternoon. Otherwise, it's a cheap place to grab a bite. ⏱ 3049 20th St at Alabama • Map G5 • (415) 648-1047 • Dis. access

7 Café Flore
Gay-central, this place, with patio seating and cozy indoor tables, is an institution (see p69). ⏱ 2298 Market St at Noe • Map F5 • (415) 621-8579 • Dis. access

8 Truly Mediterranean
This Middle Eastern snack joint is great for grabbing a bag of falafel, and a stack of pitta bread, then heading to Golden Gate Park for a picnic. ⏱ 3109 16th St • Map F5 • (415) 252-7482 • Dis. access

9 Galette
The galette refers to the buckwheat crêpes from Brittany. A very Gallic venue – sip a Belgian brew and people-watch. ⏱ 2043 Fillmore St between California & Pine • Map E3 • (415) 928-1300 • Dis. access

10 Papa Toby's Revolution Café and Artbar
Regulars nurse micro-brewed beers or their favorite coffee, and indulge in great pastries. ⏱ 3248 22nd St at Bartlett • Map F5 • (415) 642-0474

Top 10 Sunday Brunch Venues

1 Dottie's True Blue Café
A Tenderloin tradition – stand in line for the American breakfasts. ⏱ 522 Jones St • Map P3 • Dis. access

2 Sears Fine Foods
A Union Square institution, noted for its silver-dollar pancakes (see p91).

3 Ella's
Expect lines at this breakfast haven, specializing in chicken hash and banana pancakes. ⏱ 500 Presidio Ave • Map E3 • Dis. access

4 Mama's on Washington Square
The greatest French toast in town. ⏱ 1701 Stockton St • Map L4 • Dis. access

5 Miss Millie's
A favorite brunch venue with splendid fare, especially big cinnamon buns. ⏱ 4123 24th St • Map E6 • Dis. access

6 It's Tops Coffee Shop
A classic diner – their flapjacks are famously good. ⏱ 1801 Market St • Map F4

7 Kelly's Mission Rock
Enjoy the old SoMa port while eating a variety of egg-based dishes. ⏱ 817 China Basin • Map H4 • Dis. access

8 Kate's Kitchen
Huge portions of breakfast specialties, including a "French Toast Orgy". ⏱ 471 Haight St • Map F4 • Dis. access

9 Chloe's Café
Banana, walnut or pecan pancakes. ⏱ 1399 Church St at 26th • Map F6

10 The Depot
This café and bookstore is housed in an old train depot. ⏱ 87 Throckmorton Ave, Mill Valley, Marin County • Dis. access

There are several cruises each weekend around the Bay, offering champagne brunches. Telephone (415) 788-9100 for details.

Left **Vesuvio** Right **Bohemia Bar and Bistro**

🔟 Bars

1 Bubble Lounge
Right in historic Jackson Square, this very upscale, multi-roomed champagne bar features around 300 bubblies on its list. The main room is very beautiful, in a traditionally clubby sort of way *(see p90)*.

2 Bohemia Bar and Bistro
This enormous, bi-level joint has pool tables, ping-pong, a small dance floor, and a chill-out room upstairs with skylights and windows overlooking the street. The music can vary widely, depending on the DJ, from house to top-40, or you can put your money in one of the jukeboxes. ◉ *1624 California St between Polk & Van Ness • Map N1 • (415) 474-6968 • Dis. access*

3 Vesuvio
This landmark watering hole was a major Beat and hippie gathering place and attempts to carry on the alternative tradition amid the stained-glass, psyche-delic décor. Check out the literary

and other memorabilia on the walls and sit on the narrow balcony, from which you can survey the action below. ◉ *255 Columbus Ave • Map M4 • (415) 362-3370*

4 22o2 Oxygen Bar
Patrons plug into clear plastic tubes, and then breathe oxygen in through the nose and out through the mouth, available in six refreshing aromatherapy flavors. Also featured are six herb and juice cocktails served over ice, as well as sushi. ◉ *795 Valencia St at 19th • Map F5 • (415) 255-2102 • Dis. access*

5 Mecca
This dolled-up industrial space attracts some of the Castro's prettiest men, including the occasional drag queen, around the glowing circular bar, with red velvet and chiffon drapery. It's also a supper club featuring New American cuisine. ◉ *2029 Market St • Map F4 • (415) 621-7000 • Dis. access*

6 Edinburgh Castle Pub
A hugely happening place incorporating live indie music, a fish 'n' chips delivery service, as well as darts, pool, and general carousing in the Scottish manner. ◉ *950 Geary St • Map P2 • (415) 885-4074*

7 Beauty Bar
Part of a chain, this San Francisco bar opened in 1998. The interior is decorated to resemble a vintage hair salon

Bubble Lounge

Mecca

complete with hairdryers. Look out for the "manicure and martini" happy hour. The music is eclectic, and is mixed by local and nationally known DJs.
🔊 *2299 Mission St at 19th St • Map F5 • (415) 285-0323*

8 Ruby Skye
A Victorian playhouse has been restored in lavish high-tech coolness, incorporating a captivating blend of Art Nouveau and Dali-esque Modernism. And where else can you see trapeze acts on a Saturday night or puff cigars in a private billiards room? If you want to fit in, wear designer gear. 🔊 *420 Mason St • Map P3 • (415) 693-0777 • Dis. access*

9 Destino
Relax and experience the passion of flamenco and the intensity of tango every evening. Close to being under a freeway overpass, it nevertheless exudes a special energy. South American food, too. 🔊 *1815 Market St • Map F4 • (415) 552-4451 • Dis. access*

10 Lefty O'Doul's
Opened in 1958 by the local baseball legend, this Downtown landmark is a cafeteria-style sports bar with live piano music. Good fun when the old crowd starts on their renditions of even older show tunes. 🔊 *333 Geary St at Powell • Map P4 • (415) 902-8900 • Dis. access*

Top 10 San Francisco Tipples

1 Cabernet Sauvignon
This full-bodied red, with overtones of blackcurrant, is a Bay Area favorite. Try the Robert Mondavi Winery.

2 Chardonnay
Of the whites, this is the most popular, fermented in French oak barrels, lending it smooth vanilla tones. Try Sterling Vineyards *(see p32)*.

3 Other Red Wines
Pinot Noir, Merlot, and Zinfandel are giving Cabernet Sauvignon some healthy competition of late.

4 Other White Wines
Sauvignon Blanc, White Zinfandel, Chenin Blanc, and Pinot Grigio are whites that can tempt you away from the Chardonnay grape.

5 Sparkling Wines
Top French wine producers such as Mumm and Moët & Chandon have set up wineries in the Napa Valley *(see pp32–3)*.

6 Cocktails
Mojitos – white rum, ice and fresh mint – are an old standby still going strong.

7 Beers and Ales
Local breweries abound in the Bay Area, such as Anchor Steam Beer *(see p109)*.

8 Tea
A huge range of infusions, springing from the healthy attitude that dominates here.

9 Coffee
Many more ways to drink your coffee than there are in all of Europe – latte is still the blend of choice.

10 Mineral Water
The top local brand comes from, and takes its name from Calistoga in the Napa Valley.

Left **The Midnight Sun** Right **Eagle Tavern**

Gay and Lesbian Venues

The Midnight Sun
This popular, posy video bar fills up quickly after office hours and stays that way until the wee hours. Mostly good-looking 20- and 30-somethings, it's more about being admired than making connections here, so it's best to go with a friend or two, have a drink, and then move on to some livelier venue. The videos are a mix of music clips and TV sitcoms. ⓢ 4067 18th St • Map E5 • (415) 861-4186

Moby Dick
This old-time Castro hangout attracts a more mature crowd. It's generally a bunch of regulars getting together for pinball or pool – or gazing at the aquarium over the bar. The windows are big, so you can keep track of what's going down on the street. The music is largely 1980s retro that sets a fun-loving tone. ⓢ 4049 18th St • Map E5 • www.mobydicksf.com

Moby Dick

Twin Peaks
Conveniently located on the corner of Market Street, this legendary and distinctive tavern offers one of the best views of the Castro, whether by day or night. The interior is a Moroccan-style, pillowed triangular space with plate-glass windows. ⓢ 401 Castro St • Map E5 • (415) 864-9470

Eagle Tavern
Bikers and leather boys still rule at this venerable SoMa dive. Come to revel in the beer-busting, testosterone-filled atmosphere. The back patio gets going on Sunday afternoons and Thursdays feature free performances by local bands, usually grunge. ⓢ 398 12th St • Map G4 • (415) 626-0880

The Lion
The city's oldest gay bar is also its most upscale. It attracts the more yuppified denizens of the gay community who appreciate the stylish renovated Victorian in which it is housed. There's interesting music, a great fireplace, free food at Happy Hour, and hobnobbing with a wealthier clientele. ⓢ 2062 Divisadero St at Sacramento • Map E3 • (415) 567-6565

Harvey's
Named in honor of the slain gay leader Harvey Milk *(see p39)*, this is the ideal place to get to know the look and feel of

As well as the Castro District, Polk Street (see p85) is also a traditional gay area in the city.

The Lion

the Castro. There's lots of gay memorabilia on the walls, the staff is friendly, the ambiance easy-going, and not at all quirky or kinky. It's the wholesome face of gay San Francisco. ⊗ *500 Castro St at 18th • Map E5 • (415) 431-4278*

7 Martuni's
With its decor of glass and chrome and the regulars' penchant for singing old torch songs, this is a very retro piano bar for an older gay crowd. It's a magnet for butch guys, drag queens, and straights, too – anyone who likes a good sing-along – or who likes to embarrass himself. ⊗ *4 Valencia St at Market • Map F4 • (415) 241-0205*

8 Badlands
Its old, dingy interior used to live up to its menacing name, but no more since it has gone all slick and shiny. Still, it's a big draw for the under-40 set. The Sunday afternoon beer bust (4–9pm) is, for many, the most happening event of the week. ⊗ *4121 18th St • Map E5 • (415) 626-9320*

9 Café Flore
Not just a daytime cruising and coffee venue, but also by night a hopping spot. Lots of gay party people meet here first before heading out for the really late-night dancing, dark-room clubbing, and what-not that goes on all around the area *(see p65)*.

10 Lexington Club
The only full-time "girl" bar in the city, amazingly, set in a subset Mission District neighborhood that has been on the rise recently as a lesbian enclave. Young pierced sylphs, 40-something professionals, and even straight women frequent this fun "down-home, divey den for dykes," as one devotee dubbed it. ⊗ *3464 19th St at Valencia • Map F5 • (415) 863-2052*

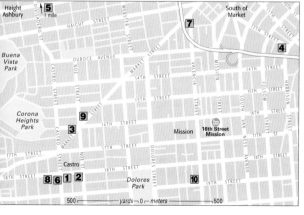

The Lexington may be the only full-time lesbian bar at present but all the male gay bars welcome women.

Left **Bambuddha Lounge** Right **Galaxy**

🔟 Nightlife

1 Bambuddha Lounge
The sumptuous restaurant in this ultra-hip nightclub serves Southeast Asian cuisine and all the dishes are priced under $15. The interior is an eclectic mix of modern slate fireplaces and floor-to-ceiling waterfalls, with a retro cocktail lounge and Asian artifacts. Bambuddha boasts a poolside dining area, and couples will enjoy the intimate corners and low tables for private conversations. ◈ *Phoenix Hotel, 601 Eddy St, between Larkin & Polk • Map Q2 • (415) 885-5088*

2 Ten 15 Folsom
Peopled mostly by wealthy young swingers with tried-and-true pickup lines, this is one of the city's most elaborate disco-extravaganzas. It features big-name DJs in a huge, SoMa multi-environment space, laid out on three levels. Don't expect anything to happen of any significance until after midnight *(see p111)*.

Ten 15 Folsom

3 Six
The terribly seedy southern Tenderloin/SoMa location can be a major drawback late at night, but once inside you can join the diverse crowd in dancing to some righteous DJs in the roomy downstairs area. The music tends toward house, trance, or whatever gets people moving. Or head upstairs to the high-ceilinged, comfortable lounge to relax and chat. ◈ *60 6th St between Market & Mission • Map Q3 • (415) 863-1221*

4 Pink
Located in a nondescript no-man's-land just on the edge of SoMa and the Mission, crowds are drawn by this club's word-of-mouth reputation. World-class DJs play here, catering to diverse audiences that enjoy music and dance. The elegant interior with flowers and white drapes adds to the ambience. ◈ *2925 16th St between Mission & South Van Ness • Map F4 • (415) 431-8889*

5 Harry Denton's Starlight Room
Something for the 40-plus set, or even 50-plus. Twenty-two stories above Union Square, couples can dance to cocktail jazz and the milder R&B hits, and relax in the easy sophistication of the place. It's 1930s-stylish, so consider it a chance to dress up in suits and party dresses, sip highballs, and enjoy the city's seductive lights. ◈ *Sir Francis Drake Hotel, 450 Powell St at Sutter • Map P4 • (415) 395-8595*

 For nightclubs in the Southern neighborhoods **See p111**

Pink

6 330 Ritch Street
Located off Townsend in this thriving SoMa area, 330 Ritch Street has been hosting events, receptions and club nights for over a decade. Known for its underground appeal, people flock to this venue for its various musical genres. ◈ *330 Ritch St at 3rd • Map R6 • (415) 541-9574*

7 The Factory
This is a spectacular "superclub," which has a different vibe almost every night, playing everything from hip-hop to salsa. There are several rooms, including the massive Blue Room, which can hold up to 500 people, and the Sky Room where weary dancers can go and chill. Although there is no official dress code, anything too casual is not encouraged. ◈ *525 Harrison St • Map 6Q • (415) 339-8686*

8 Galaxy
Just on the edge of Golden Gate Park, this is the only true dance club in Haight-Ashbury, having taken over what was one of the last remaining venues for indie bands. A busy, modern space, where DJs ply their art with a different focus every night. There are booths for cooling off in between bops. ◈ *1840 Haight St between Shrader & Stanyan • Map D4 • (415) 387-2996*

9 Metronome Ballroom
This bright Potrero Hill hall is all about dancing – dancing lessons, to be precise. Come to master the steps of the cha-cha-cha, the foxtrot, the Lindy hop, salsa, the tango, the waltz, the merengue, even break-dancing. ◈ *1830 17th St between De Haro & Rhode Island • Map G4 • (415) 252-9000*

10 Tonga Room
This Nob Hill tiki bar is almost Disneyesque in its tropical effects, including indoor monsoons and a floating band. Aimed at grown-ups of every age, it delivers kitschy Polynesian dazzlement, and is often chosen as the venue for birthday celebrations. Weekday Happy Hour (5–7pm) includes an Asian buffet at nominal cost. ◈ *Fairmont Hotel, 950 Mason St • Map N3 • (415) 772-5278*

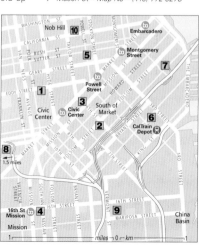

Left **Joggers in Golden Gate Park** Right **Surfers**

🔟 Outdoor Activities

1 Swimming
The icy waters of the Bay are an option only if you're a polar bear or an indomitable surfer. Most visitors will want to head for a pool – try the Embarcadero YMCA. ⓢ *Embarcadero YMCA: 169 Steuart St; (415) 957-9622 • Map H2 • www.ymcasf.org*

2 Hiking
The Bay Area is replete with magnificent hiking trails for every type of nature-lover. Land's End offers some wild terrain to scramble over *(see p117)*, and Mount Tamalpais is criss-crossed with trails *(see p124)*. But just scaling the city's hills is enough hiking for most people.

3 In-line Skating
Golden Gate Park and in-line skaters make a perfect match, especially on Sundays, when the main street in the park is closed to cars. Or try the path that runs along Marina Green for smoothly paved surfaces.

Skateboarder in Golden Gate Park

4 Skateboarding
Skateboard ramps are wherever you make them in this city – along Market Street in the Financial District, in one of the dozens of parks, or on any plaza. Protection against the inevitable vagaries of flying around on wheels means you should gear up appropriately. ⓢ *DLX: 1831 Market St; Map F4 • FTC Skateboarding: 622 Shrader St; Map D4*

5 Running
Now that Crissy Field's restoration is complete, the Golden Gate Promenade *(see p97)* is an inspiring run. And, of course, Golden Gate Park offers endless opportunities for jogging. If organized running is your thing, try the Bay to Breakers or the San Francisco Marathon. ⓢ *Bay to Breakers: 3rd Sun in May; (415) 359-2800; www.baytobreakers.com • San Francisco Marathon: Jul; (415) 284-9653 • www.runsfm.com*

6 Tennis
Free public tennis courts abound in the city. Contact the Recreation and Park Department for the one nearest you. Golden Gate Park has 21 courts, for which a small fee is charged, but you can book in advance. Most public outdoor courts are open from sunrise to sunset. Indoor courts are the purview of private tennis clubs, with membership required. ⓢ *San Francisco Recreation and Park Department: (415) 831-2700 • Golden Gate Park: (415) 753-7001*

 You can rent in-line skates from Skates on Haight, at 1818 Haight Street; tel. (415) 752-8375.

Lincoln Park Golf Course

Golf
7 The Lincoln Park 18-hole course overlooks Land's End, and Golden Gate Park has a challenging 9-hole course. The newest addition to the scene, the Presidio Golf Course, is considered one of the country's best. *Lincoln Park: (415) 221-9911 • Golden Gate Park: (415) 751-8987 • Presidio Golf Course: (415) 561-4661*

Boating
8 Sailing, rowing and kayaking are all great here, although far from a cakewalk on the Bay's unpredictable waters and sometimes ferocious prevailing winds. Play it nice and easy by taking a boat out on Stow Lake in Golden Gate Park *(see p21)*.

Extreme Sports
9 Surfing here requires great fortitude and is not for beginners. The same goes for windsurfing on the Bay. Hang-gliding can be tackled by novices under guidance. *San Francisco Hang-Gliding Center • (510) 528-2300*

Biking
10 Although the hills' amazing grades overwhelm all but those with legs of steel, bicycling is very big in San Francisco. Rent bikes from City Cycle. *City Cycle: 3001 Steiner St • (415) 346-2242 • www.citycycle.com*

Top 10 Spectator Sports

1 SF 49ers
The National Football League team strut their stuff from September to January. *3 Com Park • (415) 656-4900*

2 SF Giants
The city's baseball team plays from April to October. *SBC Park, 24 Willie Mays Plaza • (415) 972-2000*

3 Golden State Warriors
An NBA basketball team. *The Arena in Oakland, 7000 Coliseum Way, Oakland • (510) 986-2222*

4 Oakland Athletics
Members of the American Football League, and historic winners in the 1970s.

5 Oakland Raiders
Members of the American Football League.

6 Golden Gate Fields
The East Bay venue for horse-racing. *1100 East-shore Highway, Albany • (510) 559-7300*

7 Bay Meadows Racecourse
Take the CalTrain to this seasonal racetrack. *2600 S Delaware St, San Mateo • (650) 574-7223*

8 Infineon Raceway
Auto-racing. *Hwys 37 & 121, Sonoma • (707) 938-8448*

9 San Jose Sharks
Fast-paced ice hockey. *Compaq Center, West Santa Clara & Autumn Sts, San Jose • 1-800-888-2736*

10 Sacramento Monarchs
Women's basketball team. *Arco Arena, 1 Sports Parkway, Sacramento • (916) 928-3650*

Hot-air balloon flights in the Napa Valley, followed by a champagne brunch, are available; tel. 1-800-464-6824 for details.

Left **Carnaval** Right **St. Patrick's Day Parade**

🔟 Festivals and Parades

1 St. Patrick's Day Parade
With its large Irish population, not to mention the 25 or so Irish pubs scattered around town, the St. Patrick's Day Parade and the revelry that follows deep into the night is one of the city's largest celebrations. The parade journeys from 5th and Market streets to the Embarcadero. ◈ *Sun before Mar 17*

2 Cherry Blossom Festival
Japantown *(see p99)* comes spectacularly to life when the cherry trees blossom. Traditional arts and crafts, *taiko* drumming, martial arts demonstrations, and dancing, as well as delicious Japanese food make this one of the city's favorite celebrations. There's also a colorful and impressive parade. ◈ *Two weekends in Apr*

3 Cinco de Mayo
Commemorating the defeat of the French army at Puebla, Mexico, in 1862, by General Ignacio Zaragoza, this is one of the Latino community's biggest annual festivals, featuring parades, fireworks, music, and dancing. In addition to the Civic Center, much of the fun happens in the Mission District. ◈ *Sun before May 5*

4 Carnaval
Having nothing at all to do with Lent or any other traditional date, San Francisco's Carnaval is staged at the time of year when the weather will most likely be at its best for the glittery event. Groups work all year long, with the help of municipal grants, to create their dazzling costumes and put together their infectiously rhythmic routines, all to a samba, rumba, or salsa beat. ◈ *Mission District • Last weekend in May*

5 Pride Celebration Parade
More than 300,000 people attend this amazing gay event, the largest of its kind in the US, that takes over Market Street, from the Embarcadero to the Civic Center. It's up to four hours of Dykes on Bikes, drag queens in nuns' habits, leather-clad clones, gay parents, gay marching bands, muscle men, and much more. The floats – as well as the cheering throngs – are likely to be the most over-the-top, outlandish things you've ever witnessed. ◈ *Sun in late Jun*

Performer, Pride Celebration Parade

Chinese New Year

Top 10 Fairs and Gatherings

1 Haight Street Fair
You'll know hippiedom is alive and well after attending this Gathering of the Tribe. ◈ *Early Jun*

2 North Beach Festival
The city's oldest street fair features arts and crafts and some great Italian food. ◈ *Jun*

3 Fillmore Street Jazz Festival
Playing up the jazz heritage of this neighborhood, with crafts and live music. ◈ *Early Jul*

4 Renaissance Pleasure Faire
This delightful event recreates Elizabethan England, with all its ribaldry and rowdiness. ◈ *Late Aug–early Oct: Sat–Sun*

5 Burning Man
One event that defies description. It is group performance art on a behemoth scale. ◈ *1st weekend Sep*

6 Ghirardelli Square Chocolate Festival
A chocaholic's dream, with the chance to sample various nibbles. ◈ *Early Sep*

7 Folsom Street Fair
One of the biggest events for the gay community is SoMa's leather-and-body-hair carousal. ◈ *Last Sun Sep*

8 Castro Street Fair
A build-up to Hallowe'en, it focuses attention on everyday gay life. ◈ *Early Oct*

9 Tet Festival
A multicultural party, but mainly Vietnamese-American. ◈ *Jan–Feb*

10 Tribal, Folk, & Textile Arts Show
An arts and crafts fair at the Fort Mason Center, offering pottery, jewelry, textiles, and more. ◈ *Early Feb*

6 Independence Day
This waterfront festival, held from Aquatic Park to Pier 39, involves live entertainment, food stalls, and state-of-the-art fireworks launched from several points along the Bayfront. If it's foggy, the bursts of light seem that much more romantic. ◈ *Jul 4*

7 Stern Grove Festival
A much loved San Franciscan tradition, this festival showcases every kind of music you can name *(see p116)*. ◈ *Sun, early Jun–late Aug*

8 Exotic Erotic Ball
Just as outrageous as the title suggests, this indoor masquerade ball is reputedly the world's largest. ◈ *Cow Palace: 2600 Geneva Ave, Daly City • Late Oct*

9 Hallowe'en
This Castro party is a time for dress-up, dress-down, or undress, as the case may be; let your imagination run away with you as you join the gay fray. ◈ *Oct 31*

10 Chinese New Year
This is the biggest Chinese New Year celebration outside Asia. It incorporates traditional displays, and, of course, the parade of dragons and performers that winds its gaudy way through Chinatown. ◈ *Jan or Feb*

The best viewing spots for the Independence Day fireworks are Crissy Field or from Telegraph Hill – but expect large crowds.

Left **Baker Beach** Right **Half Moon Bay**

TOP10 Beaches

1 Bolinas Beach

This hidden-away Marin beach tends to be windy and is mostly used by dog-walkers, and kayakers. It's sandy, with a backdrop of rocky cliffs. If you walk north, you'll find warmer nooks and crannies out of the wind, where some sun-worshipers bask in the nude, although there is a rarely enforced city ordinance against it (see p124).

2 Stinson Beach

Three miles (5 km) of sand make this one of the most popular beaches in the Bay Area, coupled with the fact that Marin often has fine weather when the rest of the coast is covered in fog. As a result, it can be crowded when the sun comes out (see p124).

3 Muir and Red Rock Beaches

These two beaches, just south of Stinson, are the most famous nude beaches north of San Francisco. Both are sandy curves within their own coves, protected from wind and prying eyes by rocky cliffs. The only caveat is that you'll need sturdy walking shoes to get down the rough paths that lead to them from the parking lots. ◈ *Muir Beach: off Hwy 1 on Pacific Way • Red Rock: 5.5 miles (9 km) north of Muir on Pacific Way*

4 Baker Beach

This one-mile (1.5-km) stretch of sandy beach, with its perfect views of the Golden Gate Bridge, is the most popular in the city. It's great for sunbathing, dog-walking, picnicking or jogging, but signs warn off swimmers because of riptides. Sunsets here are unforgettable. ◈ *Map C2*

5 China Beach

Officially called James D. Phelan Beach, this is the poshest beach in San Francisco, being an adjunct to the exclusive Sea Cliff neighborhood. Despite its pedigree, however, California law requires that all coastal areas remain public, although access roads to them can be private. China Beach is small and protected from the wind, there's plenty of parking, and it's a pleasant walk down to the sand. Once there, you'll find showers and even changing rooms. ◈ *Map B2*

Muir Beach

Note: Swimming is not advisable at most Bay Area beaches because of the cold water and the riptides.

Land's End

6 Land's End

Although extremely beautiful in a wild, untouched way, this tiny, rocky beach is only for the hardiest nature-lovers. It's quite a hike to get here, although taking the trail up above it is quite a bit easier than going by the lower, coastal trail. Many habitués have built little sun-traps for themselves, by piling up rocks to wall-in their patches of sand *(see p115)*. ◆ *Map A3*

7 Ocean Beach

Some 4 miles (6.5 km) long and quite broad, this is the city's largest beach by far, but probably the worst for entering the water safely. It starts at Cliff House and continues on beyond the city limits, turning into picturesque dunes at the southern end. Great for walking or jogging, and when the sun comes out, it's a fine place to sunbathe *(see p115)*.

8 Half Moon Bay

About 22 miles (35 km) south of the city, the Half Moon Bay shoreline forms a long, gently curving sandy beach accessible at several points off Highway 1. A horseback riding trail runs from Dunes Beach to the bluff area of Francis Beach, and picnicking, kite-flying, surfing, and surf fishing are popular activities. ◆ *Hwy 1*

9 San Gregorio Beach

Part of San Gregorio Beach, 11.5 miles (18.5 km) south of Half Moon Bay, is clothing-optional, but it requires a good hike down the cliffs to get to. The entire stretch is partly state park, and includes a protected, driftwood-strewn estuary at the back of a wide, sandy beach, with grassy bluffs along the coast. All along there are protected areas and inlets. The estuary is home to many birds and small animals *(see p127)*.

10 Pescadero Beach

This beach has a 1-mile (1.5-km) shoreline with sandy coves, rocky cliffs, tide pools, surf-fishing spots, and picnic facilities. Across the highway is Pescadero Marsh Natural Preserve, a popular area for bird-watchers and other naturalists, being a refuge for blue heron, kites, deer, raccoons, foxes and skunks. The beach is 14.5 miles (23.3 km) south of Half Moon Bay on Highway 1 *(see p127)*.

Left **Coastal beach** Right **Monterey harbor**

TOP10 Day Trips from the City

1 Wine Country
Taking at least a day to drive up into the Napa-Sonoma hill country should be on everyone's list. Not only is the countryside beautiful, but you can also sample some of the best wines in the world, and dip into the restorative volcanic hot springs that feed the area *(see pp32–5)*.

California wine

2 Muir Woods
At the foot of Mount Tamalpais *(see p124)*, this 550-acre woodland is home to one of the few remaining first-growth groves of redwoods. The oldest of these giants is at least 1,000 years old, and such trees once covered the coastal area of California. The woods are named in honor of John Muir, the 19th-century conservationist *(see p39)*. The peace and beauty are profound. ⊗ *Muir Woods National Monument • Open 8am–sunset daily • Adm • www.nps.gov/muwo/*

Muir Woods

3 Monterey
This town is renowned for its world-class aquarium, the Monterey Jazz and Blues Festivals, and Cannery Row, made famous by author John Steinbeck, who described it as a collection of sardine canneries and whorehouses. Established by the Spanish in 1770, Monterey was the first capital of California *(see p36)* – some early buildings survive. ⊗ *Monterey Bay Aquarium: Open 9:30am–6pm daily; (831) 648-4800; Dis. access; Adm; www.mbayaq.org*

4 Big Basin State Park, Boulder Creek
Highway 9 is one of the most picturesque drives in the Bay Area, winding its way among the green Santa Cruz Mountains and through little towns where nothing much changes. Although it's minutes from Silicon Valley, life has a backwoods feel here.

5 Stanford University
Just 30 minutes south of the city, with a CalTrain depot right at the main gates, the palm-lined beauties of this campus make it worth a trip. The visual motif of sandstone and red-tile roofs has been carried forward since the Romanesque Quadrangle was built in the late 1800s. The ornate carvings that decorate the arches and pillars are extraordinarily lovely, setting off the elaborate mosaic that graces the façade of Memorial Church *(see p125)*.

The Oceanic Society conducts expeditions to the annual gray whale migration. Contact (415) 474-3385 for details.

6 Carmel

Carmel-By-The-Sea was founded as an artists' colony in the early 1900s, and is now one of the most exclusive communities in the world – having recently boasted actor Clint Eastwood as its mayor. Its old Spanish mission, one of the 21 built along the coast (see p30) is considered California's most beautiful. ◈ *Carmel Mission: 3080 Rio Rd • Open 9:30am–5:45pm Mon–Sat; 10am–5:45pm Sun • Adm • www. carmelmission.org*

Carmel Mission

7 Coastal Beaches

At least 20 different beaches line Highway 1 south of San Francisco. Some of the best include Gray Whale Cove, Montara State Beach, Miramar Beach and El Granada Beach, Roosevelt Beach, Dunes Beach, Francis Beach, Poplar Beach, Pelican Point Beach, Cowell Ranch State Beach, Martin's Beach, San Gregorio State Beach, Pescadero State Beach, Bean Hollow State Beach, and Pebble Beach.

8 Point Reyes

Some 110 sq miles (285 sq km) of pristine natural coastline make this promontory a haven for all sorts of wildlife and a thing of unforgettable, windswept beauty. You can watch whales and sea lions from Point Reyes Lighthouse (see p127).

9 Santa Cruz

This beach resort has always had a reputation for the vibrancy of its countercultural way of life. Along the beautiful coastline, the most prominent feature is the Boardwalk's Big Dipper Rollercoaster, which has been thrilling Santa Cruzers since 1923. The best swimming in the Bay Area is also here (see p127).

10 Saratoga and Los Gatos

Both of these towns, in the hills above Silicon Valley, have retained their frontier quality. One of the best things to do, other than drive the scenic roads, is to visit Hakone Gardens, a beautiful Japanese park (see p127). ◈ *Hakone Gardens: 21000 Big Basin Way, Saratoga • (408) 741-4994 • Open 10am–5pm Mon–Fri, 11am–5pm Sat–Sun • Adm • www.hakone.com*

AROUND TOWN

SAN FRANCISCO'S TOP 10

Left **Bank of California, Financial District** Right **City Hall, Civic Center**

Downtown

THE DOWNTOWN AREA IS SMALL BUT HIGHLY VARIEGATED, *including some of the city's oldest and newest landmarks, as well as some of its most exotic and eccentric neighborhoods. Colorful Chinatown, exuberant North Beach, posh Nob and Russian Hills, run-down Polk Street, the bustling Financial District, the graceful Ferry Building, and the noble architecture and cultural venues of the Civic Center – all these and more are packed into San Francisco's heart. This is where you can ride the legendary cable cars on their most scenic routes (see pp10–11), and don't forget to climb up Telegraph Hill, where Coit Tower stands as one of the city's most loved landmarks, competing successfully with the Transamerica Pyramid not far away.*

Chinatown

Sights

1. Chinatown
2. Grace Cathedral
3. North Beach
4. Nob Hill
5. Russian Hill
6. Jackson Square
7. Civic Center
8. Union Square
9. Financial District
10. Polk Street

1 Chinatown
Since its beginnings in the 1850s, this densely populated neighborhood has held its own powerful cultural identity despite every threat and cajolery. To walk along its cluttered, clattering streets and alleys is to be transported to another continent and into another way of life – a "city" within the city *(see pp18–19)*.

2 Grace Cathedral
Inspired by French Gothic architecture yet constructed of reinforced concrete, these contradictory qualities have given rise to one of the city's best-loved landmarks *(see pp24–5)*.

3 North Beach
This lively neighborhood is the city's original "Little Italy" and is still noted for its great Italian restaurants and cafés, mostly lined up along and near Columbus Avenue. In the 1950s, it was also a magnet for the Beat writers and poets, most notably Jack Kerouac and Allen Ginsberg *(see pp52–3)*, who brought to the area a Bohemian style which it still sports today. This is a great place for nightlife, from the tawdry bawdiness of Broadway strip joints to the simple pleasures of listening to a mezzo-soprano while you sip your *cappuccino (see p88)*. ⬡ Map L4

4 Nob Hill
With the advent of the cable car, San Francisco's highest hill was quickly peopled with the elaborate mansions of local magnates – in particular, the "Big Four" who built the Trans-continental railway *(see p39)* – and the

Nob Hill

name has become synonymous with wealth and power. The 1906 earthquake, however, left only one "palace" standing, now the Pacific Union Club, which still proudly dominates the center of the summit. Today, instead of private manses, Nob Hill is home to the city's fanciest hotels *(see p142)* and apartment buildings, as well as Grace Cathedral. ⬡ Map N3

5 Russian Hill
Another of San Francisco's precipitous heights, one side of which is so steep you'll find no street at all, only steps. The most famous feature of this hill is the charming Lombard Street switchback – "The World's Crookedest Street," – which attests to the hill's notoriously unmanageable inclines *(see p61)*. As with Nob Hill, with the cable car's advent, Russian Hill was claimed by the wealthy, and it maintains a lofty position in San Francisco society to this day. It supposedly took its name from the burial place of Russian fur traders, who were among the first Europeans to ply their trade at this port in the early 1800s. ⬡ Map M2

Benjamin Franklin statue, North Beach

The Making of a City

The Bay lay undiscovered by Europeans until 1769, and for years was little more than a Spanish mission village called Yerba Buena, becoming Mexican in 1821. The first great boost came when gold was discovered at Sutter's Mill in 1848. Hundreds of thousands from all over the world came to try their luck in the Gold Rush. At the same time, the US took possession of the West Coast. The Transcontinental Railway helped to firmly establish the area's financial base.

6 Jackson Square

Renovated in the 1950s, this neighborhood right next to the Transamerica Pyramid (see p46) contains some of San Francisco's oldest buildings. In the 19th century the area was notorious for its squalor, and was nick-named the "Barbary Coast," but brothels and drinking establishments have given way today to upscale offices and the city's most lavish antiques shops. The blocks around Jackson Street and Hotaling Place feature many original brick, cast-iron, and granite façades. ❧ Map M5

Jackson Square

7 Civic Center

The city's administrative center is an excellent example of grand Beaux Arts taste and illustrates San Franciscans' pride in their city (see p46). It is perhaps the most ambitious and elaborate city center complex in the US and it continues to undergo enhancements. Besides the imposing City Hall, with its vast rotunda, gold-leaf detailing, and formal gardens, the area also includes the War Memorial Opera House, the Louise M. Davies Symphony Hall, the Herbst Theater (see p56), the State Building, the New Main Library, and the monumental Old Main Library, re-inaugurated in its new incarnation as the Asian Art Museum. ❧ Map R1

8 Union Square

After 18 months of construction, this important square, which gets its name from the pro-Union rallies held here in the early 1860s, has a $25-million new look that includes performance spaces, grassy terraces, and improved parking. It is now the center for high-end shopping. Located with the edges of the Financial District on one side and the Theater District on the other (see pp50–51), it is at its most picturesque along Powell Street, where the cable cars pass right in front of the historic St Francis Hotel (see p143). The column in the center commemorates Admiral Dewey's victory at Manila Bay during the Spanish-American War of 1898. ❧ Map P4

9 Financial District

Montgomery Street, now the heart of the Financial District, was once lined with small shops where miners came to weigh their gold dust. It marks roughly

There are walking tours of the Financial District run by Hobnob Tours; call (650) 851-1123 or visit www.hobnobtours.com

First Interstate Center, Financial District

the old shoreline of shallow Yerba Buena Cove, which was filled in during the Gold Rush to create more land. Today it is lined with early 20th-century banking "temples" and modern fabrications of glass and steel. At the end of Market Street stands the newly renovated Ferry Building, which once handled 100,000 commuters a day before the city's bridges were constructed, and is now a bustling meeting spot with cafés and artisan food shops. Its tower is inspired by the Moorish belfry of Seville Cathedral in Spain. ⊗ *Map M5*

Polk Street
10 Historically, the southern part of this street, known as "Polk Gulch," was San Francisco's first openly gay district, before the rise of the Castro in the 1970s *(see p107)*. Since then it has grown shabbier, although it still attracts plenty of younger gays to its clubs, bars, and shops. At the other end, just down from Russian Hill, Polk Street is one of the city's shopping and dining lures, with a host of fine choices to tempt the eyes and palates of a discerning clientele. ⊗ *Map Q1*

A Walk Around North Beach

Morning

Start at the top of North Beach, on **Telegraph Hill** *(see p88)*, admire the famous views, and visit **Coit Tower** *(see p46)*, making sure to take in the murals. Next, walk down to **Filbert Street** *(see p88)* and go right a couple of blocks until you get to lovely **Washington Square**, where, at **Saints Peter and Paul Catholic Church**, Marilyn Monroe and local baseball great Joe DiMaggio had their wedding pictures taken *(see p88)*. Continue on along Columbus Avenue to the left and pay a visit at colorful **Caffè Roma** *(see p90)*, where you can indulge in a bit of sidewalk ogling. Or, across the street, pay homage to the time-honored **US Restaurant** *(see p91)* which serves some of the best pasta in town.

Afternoon

After lunch, take a left on Green Street and go over one block to **Upper Grant** *(see p88)*, with its funky shops and bars, a regular hangout since the 1950s. Turn right on to Vallejo Street, where a visit to the famous **Caffè Trieste** *(see p90)* for a coffee and the authentic Bohemian atmosphere is a must. Continue on down Columbus to William Saroyan Place and at No. 12 you'll find Specs', an exuberant bar filled with Beat memorabilia. Finally, just across Columbus at No. 261 is the immortal **City Lights Bookstore** *(see p88)*, where you can browse the Beat poetry written by owner Lawrence Ferlinghetti and friends.

Following pages: **Chinese New Year parade, Chinatown**

Left **City Lights Bookstore** Right **Filbert Street Steps**

10 North Beach Sights

1 Telegraph Hill
Named after the semaphore installed on its crest in 1850, the hill's eastern side was dynamited to provide rocks for landfill. Steps descend its slopes, lined with gardens. At its summit stands Coit Tower. ✆ *Map L5*

2 North Beach Views
The panoramic views from both the hill and the top of the Coit Tower are justly celebrated. The wide arc sweeping from the East Bay and the Bay Bridge to Alcatraz and the Golden Gate Bridge is breathtaking.

3 Coit Tower Murals
The frescoes were painted by local artists in 1934, to provide jobs during the Depression *(see p47)*. The murals are socio-political commentary yet are also appealing for their details of life in California at the time. ✆ *Map L5*

4 Filbert Street Steps
The flowery descent down these rustic steps provides great views of the Bay. ✆ *Map L5*

5 City Lights Bookstore
The Beat poet Lawrence Ferlinghetti founded City Lights in 1953. It's a great place to leaf through a few volumes of poetry or the latest free papers to find out what's on. ✆ *261 Columbus Ave • Map M4 • (415) 362-8193*

6 Broadway
Made famous in the 1960s for its various adult entertain-ments, the offerings haven't changed much. Enrico's, at No. 504, is a great place for dinner *(see p91)*. ✆ *Map M5*

7 Upper Grant
Saloons, cafés, and bluesy music haunts give this northerly section of Grant Avenue a very alternative feel. ✆ *Map L4*

8 Caffè Trieste
If you're in the quarter on a Saturday afternoon, don't miss the impromptu opera that takes place here. But any time is right for this artists' and writers' gathering place *(see p90)*.

9 Washington Square
This pretty park is lined with Italian bakeries, restaurants and bars. Don't be surprised to see practitioners of *t'ai chi* doing their thing on the lawn every morning. ✆ *Map L4*

10 Saints Peter & Paul Church
Neo-Gothic in conception, with an Italianesque façade, this church is also called the Italian Cathedral and the Fisherman's Church, since many Italians who originally lived in the neighbor-hood made their living by fishing *(see p45)*. ✆ *666 Filbert St • Map L4 • Open daily • Free*

Coit Tower

There are guided tours of North Beach's Italian and Beat history, food and culture. Contact the tourist office (see p132) for details.

Left **Serge Sorokko Gallery** Right **W. Graham Arader III**

🔟 Downtown Shopping

1 Shreve & Co
A San Francisco original and one of the city's most elegant jewelers. In addition to gems set in wonderful ways, you'll also find fine timepieces, Limoges porcelain, and Lalique crystal. ⊗ *200 Post St at Grant • Map P4 • (415) 421-2600 • Dis. access*

2 W. Graham Arader III
One of Jackson Square's most appealing shops is like an art museum, featuring fine antique prints. You can marvel at Audubon's *Birds of America*, ancient maps, and historic works. ⊗ *435 Jackson St, Jackson Square • Map M5 • (415) 788-5115 • Dis. access*

3 Wilkes Bashford
A San Francisco institution for deluxe apparel by up-and-coming local and international designers. ⊗ *375 Sutter St • Map P4 • (415) 986-4380 • Dis. access*

4 Jeanine Payer
An innovative jewelry designer with a strong celebrity following who creates pieces that combine Old World craftsmanship with contemporary design. ⊗ *760 Market St • Map P4 • Dis. access*

5 Serge Sorokko Gallery
If you're in the market for something by one of the modern masters, this is an excellent place to browse. Important prints and other works by Picasso, Matisse, Miró, Chagall, and other 20th-century greats, such as Tapiès, Bacon, and Warhol. ⊗ *231 Grant Ave • Map P4 • (415) 421-7770*

6 Christopher-Clark Fine Art
Another gallery for modern European masters. A good stock of Bay Area artists, too. ⊗ *320 Geary St • Map P4 • (415) 397-7781 • Dis. access*

7 Aria
This hideaway is loaded with collectibles of all sorts. You're likely to discover anything from an old Buddha to an Art Deco lamp. ⊗ *1522 Grant Ave • Map L4 • (415) 433-0219 • Dis. access*

8 The North Face
Another San Francisco original, here you'll find everything for the outdoor adventurer. ⊗ *180 Post St • Map P4 • (415) 433-3223 • Dis. access*

9 Wingard
If you like the decor of your hotel, chances are some of the touches have been supplied by this company. Lamps, bathroom accessories, and home accents at wholesale prices. ⊗ *2127 Union St • Map F2 • (415) 345-1999 • Dis. access*

10 New India Bazaar
A long-time local favorite for every sort of Indian-Pakistani spice and foodstuff. They also carry an array of Hindu religious artifacts and Indian videos. ⊗ *1107 Polk St • Map P1 • (415) 928-4553*

Check out the jewelry designs of Jeanine Payer at www.jeaninepayer.com

Left **Grand Café** Right **Tosca**

Cafés and Bars

1 Caffè Trieste
One of the most authentic cafés in town, rich with arty non-chalance *(see p64)*. ◎ *605 Vallejo St • Map M4 • (415) 392-6739 • Dis. access*

2 Tosca
Dating back to 1919, this North Beach bar is a favorite with celebrities. The jukebox plays opera arias. ◎ *242 Columbus Ave • Map M4 • Closed L • (415) 391-1244 • Dis. access*

3 Caffè Roma
You're as likely to hear Italian here as you are English, not only from the staff but from the patrons. A friendly atmosphere in which to enjoy an *espresso* and eye passers-by. ◎ *526 Columbus Ave • Map L4 • (415) 296-7662 • Dis. access*

4 O'Reilly's
The bar dates from 1825 and was imported from Ireland. Every-thing here evokes the Emerald Isle. ◎ *622 Green St at Columbus • Map L4 • (415) 989-6222 • Dis. access*

5 Grand Café
A stylish place to see and be seen, as an addendum to the chic Hotel Monaco. ◎ *501 Geary St at Taylor • Map P3 • (415) 292-0101 • Dis. access*

6 Quetzal
A colorful, bustling place where you can get a brew – from coffee to beer – and check your e-mail. Breakfast and lunch fare. ◎ *1234 Polk St at Bush • Map N1 • (415) 673-4181 • Dis. access*

7 Bambuddha Lounge
This popular and trendy restaurant and nightclub is the place to visit for fabulous cocktails and hip beats. There is a heated patio *(see p70)*.

8 Bubble Lounge
A champagne bar with room after room of subdued lighting and cozy corners *(see p66)*. ◎ *714 Montgomery St • Map M5 • (415) 434-4204 • Dis. access*

9 Red Room
All red and tiny, as the name implies, this joint lures devotees with its classic cocktails. ◎ *Next door to Commodore Hotel, 827 Sutter St between Jones and Leavenworth • Map P2 • (415) 346-7666 • Dis. access*

10 The Irish Bank
Down a picturesque alley, this winning pub feels very Irish. Tip a Guinness before the 5pm yuppie rush to get the best taste of its friendly vibes. ◎ *10 Mark Lane, off Bush St • Map P4 • (415) 788-7152*

Price Categories

For a three-course meal for one with half a bottle of wine (or equivalent meal), taxes and extra charges.	
$	under $20
$$	$20–$40
$$$	$40–$55
$$$$	$55–$80
$$$$$	over $80

Above **Enrico's**

🔟 Places to Eat

1 The Dining Room

The setting, the service, and the food all live up to the Ritz name *(see p62)*. ◊ Ritz-Carlton Hotel, 600 Stockton Street • Map P4 • (415) 773-6198 • Dis. access • $$$$$

2 Tommy Toy's Haute Cuisine Chinoise

This elegant institution serves marvelous fare in a sumptuous setting. The cuisine is a melding of Chinese and French. ◊ 655 Montgomery St • Map N5 • (415) 397-4888 • Dis. access • $$$$

3 Rubicon

A chic environment in which to enjoy some of the city's best cuisine and wines. California-French in inspiration *(see p62)*. ◊ 558 Sacramento St • Map N5 • (415) 434-4100 • Closed Sun • Dis. access • $$$$

4 One Market

The views of the Bay's lights are spectacular at night, and the food memorable. ◊ 1 Market St at Steuart • Map N6 • (415) 777-5577 • Closed Sun • Dis. access • $$$$

5 Enrico's

Considering it's mostly a café for people-watching, the food is wonderful – try the stuffed fried olives. ◊ 504 Broadway • Map M5 • (415) 982-6223 • Dis. access • $$

6 US Restaurant

Everything served here is simple and authentically Italian. ◊ 515 Columbus Ave • Map L4 • (415) 397-5200 • $$

7 Capp's Corner

Serves one of the most authentic minestrones outside of Italy. ◊ 1600 Powell St • Map L4 • (415) 989-2589 • Dis. access • $$

8 Sears Fine Food

This 1950s retro coffee shop is always good for a quick fill-up *(see p65)*. ◊ 439 Powell St • Map P4 • (415) 986-1160 • Closed Tue–Wed • Dis. access • $

9 Clown Alley

Solid American diner food – burgers, hot dogs, French fries, shakes, and wine and beer, too. ◊ 42 Columbus Ave • Map M5 • (415) 421-2540 • No credit cards • Dis. access • $

10 Ponzu

This Asian-style tapas restaurant, with bar, has an eclectic choice of pan-Asian cuisine served on small plates – perfect for sharing. ◊ 401 Taylor Street • Map P3 • (415) 775-7979 • Closed L • $$$

Note: Unless otherwise stated, all restaurants accept credit cards and serve vegetarian meals

Left **Logo, Fort Mason Center** Right **Hyde Street Pier, The Embarcadero**

The North Shoreline

AS ITS NAME SUGGESTS, the Bayshore area spreads out along the Bay at the northern edge of the city, faces the islands, and enjoys unforgettable views of both the Bay and Golden Gate Bridges. Historically, the city began its life here, when the Spanish set up a military outpost at the Presidio in 1776. More history can be found at the piers of the northern Embarcadero, including now heavily commercialized Pier 39 and Fisherman's Wharf, where San Francisco's fishing industry began in the 19th century. But also part of the area is the smart Marina District, with its swanky homes and two yacht clubs. Some of the finest parks are found here too, most notably the Presidio, Crissy Field, the Marina Green, and the Great Meadow above the Fort Mason Center. A particularly stylish remnant of the 1915 Panama-Pacific Exposition is also found here – the Neo-Classical Palace of Fine Arts – with its hands-on science museum annex, the Exploratorium.

Ferry Building, Embarcadero

10 Sights

1. Golden Gate Bridge
2. Fisherman's Wharf
3. Alcatraz
4. Angel, Treasure, and Yerba Buena Islands
5. The Embarcadero
6. Fort Mason Center
7. Marina District
8. Palace of Fine Arts and the Exploratorium
9. Crissy Field
10. The Presidio

Golden Gate Bridge

1 Golden Gate Bridge

This world-famous engineering masterpiece sets off the entrance to San Francisco Bay in the most spectacular way, and never fails to elicit gasps of awe from first-time visitors and old-timers alike *(see pp8–9)*.

2 Fisherman's Wharf

Although now largely tourist-oriented, there are still authentic sights to see, aromas to savor, and salt air to breathe among these piers *(see pp12–13)*.

3 Alcatraz

America's "Devil's Island" didn't operate as a prison for very long, but it can still evoke a chill *(see pp14–17)*.

4 Angel, Treasure, and Yerba Buena Islands

A trip out to Angel Island, now a state park, can make for a very pleasant day of picnicking, biking, hiking, kayaking, and swimming. But in the early 1900s it was the "Ellis Island of the West," where would-be immigrants, mostly Chinese, could be detained for months. During World War II, it served as a prisoner of war camp and later as a missile base. Treasure Island was built in 1939 for the Golden Gate International Exposition and was a US Navy base during World War II; it is now once again owned by the city and has recently become San Francisco's newest suburb. Yerba Buena Island is a Coast Guard station and is mostly closed to visitors. ⚓ *Ferries from Pier 41*

5 The Embarcadero

The Embarcadero starts at Aquatic Park and curves all the way around to Hunters Point at the southeastern edge of the city. Now that the Port of Oakland handles the Bay's shipping needs, the old piers are used for any number of purposes these days, and the parallel road has recently become a park promenade *(see p49)*. Pier 39 is the most famous since it was turned into an amusement attraction in the 1980s, while other piers house concerts, festivals, antiques fairs, and restaurants. When looking for a particular pier, note that those to the north of the Ferry Building have odd numbers and those to the south, even. ⚓ *Map G1*

Sea lions on Pier 39, Fisherman's Wharf

Around Town – The North Shoreline

View of the Marina District

6 Fort Mason Center

Formerly a military base established during the Civil War, some of the army buildings have been devoted to cultural programs of all kinds since 1976. Some 50 organizations now call it home, including museums, art galleries, theaters, shops, festivals, fairs, and performance spaces, as well as libraries and various institutes. Some of the most prominent are the Museum of Craft and Folk Art and the Museo Italo-Americano (see p42), the San Francisco African-American Historical and Cultural Society, the Children's Art Theater, the Magic Theater (see p57), and Herbst Pavilion. The city's finest vegetarian restaurant, Greens, is also located here, enjoying unique views of the Bay and Golden Gate (see p97). ◈ Map F1

7 Marina District

This is a pleasant, upmarket zone, featuring bars and trendy boutiques along Chestnut Street. Marina Green is a vast lawn where locals love to jog, skate, fly kites, picnic, or walk their dogs. At the tip of the break-water that protects the Marina, you can tune in to the bizarre sounds of the Wave Organ, an instrumental structure of underwater pipes through which the tides slosh in a vaguely musical fashion. ◈ Map E1

8 Palace of Fine Arts and the Exploratorium

The sole survivor – with a lot of help from restorers – of the many fantasy monuments built for the 1915 Panama-Pacific Exposition, the Neo-Classical Palace was an Expo' center-piece. The dome of the rotunda is supported by a Classical frieze and an octagonal arcade, which is set off by a landscaped lagoon and flanked by an open peristyle of Corinthian columns (see p46). Behind it is the Exploratorium, one of the world's first hands-on science museums. It boasts more than 650 exhibits, divided into 13 subject areas, such as Electricity, Motion, Weather, Vision, Color and Light, and Sound (see p58). ◈ 3601 Lyon St • Map E1 • (415) EXP-LORE; general info. (415) 561-0360 • Open 10am–5pm Tue–Sun • Adm • www.exploratorium.edu

9 Crissy Field

Originally marshland and dunes, the field was filled in for the 1915 Pan-Pacific Exposition and paved over entirely for use as an airfield by the army from 1919–36. With the establishment

94

For information on the full range of events offered at the Fort Mason Center during your visit, go to www.fortmason.org

of the Presidio as a national park under the supervision of the city, a massive restoration project has now returned part of Crissy Field to wetlands and the rest to lawns, pathways, and picnic areas. The city's 100-acre "Front Yard" is one of the prime viewing sites for the July 4 fireworks displays, while the Golden Gate Promenade is a 3-mile (5-km) paved pathway that runs through this district from Aquatic Park to Fort Point. ◈ Map D1

The Presidio

10 This beautiful wooded corner of the city has stunning views over the Golden Gate, but from 1776 until 1994 it was owned and occupied by first the Spanish, then the Mexican, and finally, the US armies, and almost entirely off-limits to anyone else. It has now been dubbed a major part of the Golden Gate National Recreational Area, and plans are still coalescing as to its ultimate future. At the very least, it is a spectacular park, full of nature trails, streams, forests, drives, and historic structures. Some of the buildings are being turned into cultural centers, but many of them are still residences. Parts of it may eventually be developed for commercial use (see p48). ◈ Map D2

Presidio Officers' Club, The Presidio

A Bike Ride through the Presidio

Beginning at the Visitor Information Center, where you can pick up an excellent map, first explore the Main Post. Here you can ride around the Parade Ground, see the Presidio's earliest surviving buildings, dating from the 1860s, as well as 18th-century Spanish adobe wall fragments in the former Officers' Club.

Exit the area on Sheridan, which takes you past the Spanish Colonial Revival-style Golden Gate Club, and turn left onto Lincoln, which winds around the National Military Cemetery. Turn right on McDowell; on the left you see the Colonial Revival Cavalry Barracks. The African-American "Buffalo Soldiers" were stationed here from 1902 to 1904.

Now go past the five brick Stables, off to both the left and the right, and stop at the quirky Pet Cemetery on the left, where post guard dogs are buried, and also family pets. Next, head under Highway 101 to encounter Stilwell Hall, built in 1921 as enlisted barracks and a mess hall for the airmen; turn left to take in the metal Aerodrome Hangars from the same era; then proceed on and pause at **Crissy Field** to admire the views.

Double back at this point, take the next left down toward the Bay and join the Golden Gate Promenade all the way out to Fort Point where you can experience the **Golden Gate Bridge** (see pp8–9) and the crashing waves of the Pacific up close and personal.

For bike rentals **See p134**. The Presidio visitor center is now temporarily located in the Presidio Officers' Club until 2005.

95

Left **Ghirardelli chocolate bars** Right **Cost Plus World Market**

🔟 Wharf Area Shops

1 Ghirardelli Chocolate
Stop by for a free sample and then stock up on your mouth-watering favorites. If you're feeling nostalgic take home some chocolate cable cars. ⬡ *Ghirardelli Square, 900 North Point St • Map K2 • (415) 775-5500*

2 Operetta
As fine a collection of Italian handmade pottery as you are likely to see this side of the Atlantic. Delightful works from Sicily, Umbria, and Tuscany. ⬡ *Ghirardelli Square, 900 North Point St • Map K2 • (415) 928-4676*

3 Destinations
A travel clothing store geared towards adventure, business travel and city treks. It stocks brands such as Helly Hansen, The North Face, and Ex Officio. ⬡ *Ghirardelli Square, 815 Beach St • Map K2 • (415) 441-4177*

4 Russian Treasure
A delightful shop specializing in all that is colorful and whimsical from Old Russia, including the famous nested dolls. ⬡ *The Cannery, 2nd Floor, 2801 Leavenworth St • Map J2 • (415) 346-1104*

5 Golden Gate National Parkstore
This shop is a buried treasure amid all the hoopla of the Wharf area. All the information you need for visiting the Bay Area's parks, plus great little souvenirs. ⬡ *Pier 39 • Map J4 • (415) 433-7221*

6 N.F.L. Shop
Officially licensed to sell products for all major league sports, so here's your chance to stock up on the jerseys and caps of all your favorite teams. ⬡ *Pier 39, Ground Level • Map J4 • (415) 397-2027*

7 Collectibles of Asia
In a complete departure from the usual kitsch of Pier 39, this shop offers genuine Chinese antiques at very affordable prices. You can find carvings, masterful ceramics, and much more. ⬡ *Pier 39, 2nd Floor, Building P, No. 214 • Map J4*

8 Elegant Illusions
A glittering range of lab-created gemstone jewelry. The collection includes specialty jewelry for children. ⬡ *900 North Point • Map K2 • (415) 398-1922*

9 Cost Plus World Market
The original world import mart that set the trend for all the others. It can still surprise with a well-chosen item from some far-away land. ⬡ *2552 Taylor St • Map K3 • (415) 928-6200*

10 Book Bay Bookstore
Great secondhand books, records, and CDs, and all the proceeds support programs in San Francisco's libraries. No better prices anywhere. ⬡ *Fort Mason Center, Building C • Map F1 • (415) 771-1076*

Price Categories

For a three-course meal for one with half a bottle of wine (or equivalent meal), taxes and extra charges.

$	under $20
$$	$20–$40
$$$	$40–$55
$$$$	$55–$80
$$$$$	over $80

Above **McCormick & Kuleto's**

Places to Eat

1 Gary Danko
The French-American menu allows you to create your own mix 'n' match fixed-price selection. If you don't have a reservation, head for the bar, where you can order anything on the menu. ◎ 800 North Point St at Hyde • Map K2 • (415) 749-2060 • Dis. access • $$$$$

2 Alioto's
This first-rate restaurant serves Sicilian and seafood dishes in an old-style interior. There are great views over the Golden Gate Bridge. ◎ 8 Fisherman's Wharf • Map J4 • (415) 673-0183 • Dis. access • $$$$

3 Ana Mandara
An exotic eatery with a touch of Las Vegas pizzazz. The food is Indo-Chinese and delicious. ◎ 891 Beach St at Polk • Map K1 • (415) 771-6800 • Dis. access • $$$

4 Isa
The tiny dining room of this Marina discovery is also the kitchen. The concept is nouvelle French tapas, so portions are petite but exquisite. ◎ 3324 Steiner St between Chestnut and Lombard • Map E2 • (415) 567-9588 • Dis. access • $$$

5 McCormick & Kuleto's
Come for the view; stay for the chilled seafood sampler. ◎ Ghirardelli Sq, 900 North Point St • Map K2 • (415) 929-1730 • Dis. access • $$

6 Greens
For two decades, Greens has carried the banner of vegetarianism in the Bay Area. Inventive dishes plus panoramas add up to a treat (see p62). ◎ Fort Mason Center, Buchanan St, Building A • Map F1 • (415) 771-6222 • Dis. access • $$$

7 The Mandarin
Opened in 1968, Northern Chinese cuisine is served in this popular restaurant with fine Bay Area views. ◎ Ghirardelli Sq, 900 North Point St • Map K2 • (415) 673-8812 • $$

8 Scoma's
A Fisherman's Wharf seafood tradition since 1965 (see p12). Enjoy the cracked crab roasted in garlic and olive oil.

9 Grandeho's Kamekyo
Japanese food at its best. Sushi of all sorts. ◎ 2721 Hyde St between Beach and North Point • Map K2 • (415) 673-6828 • Dis. access • $$$

10 The Buena Vista Café
This café claims to have invented Irish coffee. The menu features American standards. ◎ 2765 Hyde St • Map K2 • (415) 474-5044 • Dis. access • $$

Note: Unless otherwise stated, all restaurants accept credit cards and serve vegetarian meals

Left **Union Street** Right **Golden Gate Park**

Central Neighborhoods

*A*S WITH EVERY QUADRANT OF SAN FRANCISCO, *diversity is the keynote here. This area encompasses the oldest money and the highest society of the city's founding families, as well as some of the poorest of citizens. It takes in the staunchest pillars of the politically savvy – though true conservatives are a rarity in this progressive city – as well as the wildest let-it-all-hang-out free-thinkers. Then, too, there's a considerable swathe of the comfortably middle-class who, like all San Franciscans, are simply intent on enjoying the beauties and pleasures of their great city.*

Sights and Neighborhoods

1. Golden Gate Park
2. Union Street
3. Pacific Heights
4. Japantown
5. Haight-Ashbury
6. Hayes Valley
7. Geary Boulevard
8. Presidio Heights
9. Western Addition
10. The Richmond District

Spreckels Mansion

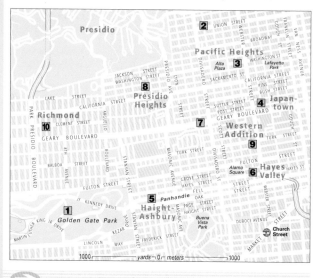

1 Golden Gate Park
One of the largest, finest parks-cum-cultural centers in world. No visit to the city is complete without taking in some of its wonders *(see pp20–23)*.

2 Union Street
A neighborhood shopping street loaded with tradition, Union Street is noted for its sidewalk cafés, antiques shops, bookstores, and designer boutiques, housed in converted Victorian charmers. The street is at the heart of the Cow Hollow neighborhood, whose name invokes its antecedent as a dairy pasture *(see p51)*. ✎ *Map E2*

3 Pacific Heights
A grander, more exclusive residential area is hard to imagine. Commanding as it does heights up to 300 ft (100 m) overlooking the magnificent Bay, everything about it proclaims power and wealth. The blocks between Alta Plaza and Lafayette Park are the very heart of the area, but the grandeur extends from Gough to Divisadero and beyond. On a sunny day, there's nothing more exhilarating than scaling its hills and taking in the perfectly manicured streets, the

Typical house, Pacific Heights

Japantown

to-die-for views, and the palatial dwellings. The Spreckels Mansion, a limestone palace in the Beaux-Arts tradition, on Washington and Octavia streets, is the brightest gem of the lot, now owned by novelist Danielle Steele *(see p53)*. ✎ *Map E2*

4 Japantown
The Japan Center was built as part of an ambitious 1960s plan to revitalize the Fillmore District. Blocks of aging Victorians were demolished and replaced by the Geary Express-way and this Japanese-style shopping complex, with a five-tiered, 75-ft (22-m) Peace Pagoda at its heart. Taiko drummers perform here during the Cherry Blossom Festival each April *(see p74)*. The extensive malls are lined with authentic Japanese shops and restaurants, plus an eight-screen cinema, and the Kabuki Springs and Spa. More shops and restaurants are found along the outdoor mall across Post Street. This neighborhood has been the focus of the Japanese community for some 75 years. ✎ *Map F3*

Positively Haight Street, Haight-Ashbury

5 Haight-Ashbury

This anarchic quarter is one of the most scintillating and unconventional in the city, resting firmly on its laurels as ground zero for the worldwide Flower-Power explosion of the 1960s *(see p55)*. Admire the beautiful old Queen Anne-style houses, a few of them still painted in the psychedelic pigments of that hippie era. There are still some tripping freaks and neo-Flower Children here, along with far-out shops and the venerable Haight Ashbury Free Clinic. Groove along the street and recreate your own "Summer of Love." The Lower Haight is noted for its edgy clubs and bars. ✆ *Map D4*

Flower Power

In 1967 San Francisco witnessed the Summer of Love, including a 75,000-strong Human Be-In at Golden Gate Park. People were drawn here – many with flowers in their hair – by the acid-driven melodies of Jefferson Airplane, Janis Joplin, Jimi Hendrix, and The Doors. Love was free, concerts were free, drugs were free, even food and healthcare were free. Soon, however, public alarm, and too many bad trips, caused the bubble to burst.

---

6 Hayes Valley

Rising like a phoenix from the ashes of racial unrest in what used to be a very rundown African-American slum, this small area has now become one of San Francisco's hipper shopping and dining districts. The dismantling of an ugly freeway overpass following the 1989 earthquake helped turn the tide, along with the razing of a housing project nearby. The result is a chic area that hasn't lost its edge. Hayes Valley festivals occur at midsummer and Christmas, when the streets are thronged with revelers. ✆ *Map F4*

7 Geary Boulevard

One of the city's main traffic arteries, sweeping from Van Ness all the way out to Cliff House, is a typically unprepossessing urban thoroughfare, but functional. It begins its journey at Market Street, sweeps past Union Square, and then forms the heart of the Theater District, before venturing into the notorious Tenderloin, home to seedy clubs and sex-workers. After it crosses Van Ness, it zips past Japantown and the funky Fillmore District. Soon you're in the Richmond District and before you know it, there's the Pacific Ocean. ✆ *Map F3*

8 Presidio Heights

Originally part of the "Great Sand Waste" to the west, this neighborhood is now one of the most élite. The zone centers on Sacramento Street as its discreet shopping area. It's worth a stroll, primarily for the architecture. Of interest are the Swedenborgian Church at 2107 Lyon Street, the Roos House at 3500 Jackson Street, and Temple Emanu-El at 2 Lake Street. ✆ *Map D3*

9 Western Addition

This area, too, was once sandy waste, but after World War II the district became populated by Southern African-Americans who came west for work. For a short time, it was famous for jazz and blues clubs, as embodied, until his death in 2001, by John Lee Hooker and his Boom Boom Room. Today, it is still largely African-American in character and rather rundown, although it does comprise architecturally odd St Mary's Cathedral (see p44) and photogenic Alamo Square (see p49). 🔊 Map E3

10 The Richmond District

This flat district of row houses begins at Masonic Street, sandwiched between Golden Gate Park and California Street. It ultimately extends all the way to the Pacific Ocean, being more and more prone to stay fog-bound the farther west you go. The district is very ethnically diverse and resoundingly middle class. Over the decades, it has been settled by White Russians, East European Jews, and most recently Chinese-Americans and another wave of Russians. 🔊 Map C3

Russian shop, Richmond District

A Hippie Tour of Haight-Ashbury

Begin at **Alamo Square** (see p49), with the Westerfield House at 1998 Fulton at Scott, former residence of Ken Kesey, the writer and visionary who arguably got the whole 1960s movement going. Walk up Scott, turn right on Page and go to No. 1090, where Big Brother and the Holding Company got their start. A block and a half farther on, go right on Lyon to No. 112, where Janis Joplin lived for most of 1967 (see p55).

Continue on to the Pan-handle, an extension of Golden Gate Park, where in June 1967 the Jimi Hendrix Experience gave a free concert. Now turn left on Central and head up to steep **Buena Vista Park** (see p49), site of public Love-Ins in the 1960s and 1970s. Turn right on Haight and check out Positively Haight Street, 1400 Haight Street at Masonic, one of the fanciest hippie shops.

Continue on to the famous Haight-Ashbury intersection and walk along Haight to Clayton; at No. 558 is the much-loved Haight Ashbury Free Clinic, still imbued with the spirit of the 1960s. Savor a well-earned *cappuccino* and snack at the **People's Cafe** (see p105).

Refreshed, walk towards the park, turn right on Stanyan all the way to Fulton. At 2400 Fulton stands the former Jefferson Airplane Mansion, which used to be painted black. Finally, head back to **Golden Gate Park** (see pp20–23) and make your way to Hippie Hill to groove to the tribal drums.

Following pages: **Victorian Conservatory, Golden Gate Park**

Left **Enchanted Crystal** Right **John Wheatman & Associates**

Shops

Around Town – Central Neighborhoods

1 John Wheatman & Associates
Understated, somewhat Oriental elegance in warm, cozy tones is what this showroom is all about. If you're not in the market for antiques or designer furniture, stop by for their subtle pottery or paintings. ⊗ 1933 Union St • Map F2 • (415) 346-8300

2 Enchanted Crystal
This gallery/store offers an amazing collection of art, glass, handcrafted jewelry, and decorative gifts. ⊗ 1895 Union St • Map F2 • (415) 885-1335

3 Carol Doda's Champagne & Lace Lingerie Boutique
Bodywear for women and men, brought to you by the infamous entertainment pioneer who brought topless dancing to San Francisco in the 1960s. Naturally, the emphasis is on risqué styles. ⊗ 1850 Union St • Map F2 • (415) 776-6900

4 Brooks Shoes For Kids
This store specializes in high fashion with a huge range in all styles. Accessories and toys are also sold here. ⊗ 3307 Sacramento St • Map E3 • (415) 440-7599

5 Worldware
This luxurious collection of home furnishings, gifts, and accessories from around the world is the love-child of an interior design couple. ⊗ 336 Hayes St • Map F4 • (415) 487-9030

6 Polanco
A sophisticated gallery of Mexican arts, featuring silver jewelry, carved and painted figures of saints, as well as the work of emerging Mexican artists. ⊗ 393 Hayes St • Map F4 • (415) 252-5753

7 L'Art Deco Français
This is the US branch of a remarkable collection of French furniture and *objets d'art* from the 1920s to the 1950s. On display are tables, lamps, iron-works, ceramics, glass, paintings, sculptures, and more. ⊗ 1680 Market St • Map F4 • (415) 863-5483

8 Comix Experience
Comics with adult aficiona-dos in mind: *The Ring of the Nibelung*, *The Filth*, *Naughty Bits*, *Static-X*, *Peculia*, and *Auto-matic Kafka* are just a few of the whacky titles awaiting you in new and vintage issues. ⊗ 305 Divisadero St • Map E4 • (415) 863-9258

9 Forever After Books
Perhaps the funkiest used bookstore in the world. There are piles of tomes stacked on every surface, but the owners know where to find just about anything you're looking for. ⊗ 1475 Haight St • Map E4 • (415) 431-8299

10 Amoeba Music
Besides thousands of LPs, tapes, and CDs, there's also a huge selection of videos and posters. ⊗ 1855 Haight St • Map D4 • (415) 831-1200

Above **Absinthe**

Price Categories

For a three-course meal for one with half a bottle of wine (or equivalent meal), taxes and extra charges.	**$** under $20
	$$ $20–$40
	$$$ $40–$55
	$$$$ $55–$80
	$$$$$ over $80

🔟 Places to Eat

1 Perry's
A San Francisco institution, noted for its burgers and other all-American faves, including meatloaf, prime rib, and fried chicken. ◎ 1944 Union St • Map F2 • (415) 922-9022 • Dis. access • $$

2 Aldis
Vibrant, colorful dishes based on Mediterranean cuisine from Italy, Spain, and the Middle East. An extensive wine list and full bar. ◎ 2000 Union St • Map F2 • (415) 563-3305 • Dis. access • $$

3 Yoshida-Ya
One of the old-standby Japanese choices. Although the sushi is remarkable, it's the yakitori (barbecue) that gives the place its ongoing reputation. ◎ 2909 Webster St • Map E2 • (415) 346-3431 • Dis. access • $$

4 The Grove
It almost feels like a mountain lodge, with lounging furniture and roaring fire. The tempting menu offers tasty entrées such as chicken pot pie or three-cheese macaroni. ◎ 2016 Fillmore St • Map E3 • (415) 474-1419 • Dis. access • $$

5 Miyako
The Japantown Mall is designed to resemble a typical Japanese village. This restaurant offers all Japanese delights, including udon (noodles in broth). ◎ Japantown, 1707 Buchanan Mall • Map F3 • (415) 567-6552 • $$

6 Absinthe
Like being air-lifted to a Paris bistro. Specials such as confit of Muscovy duck leg with prunes, Landais potatoes, and arugula. ◎ 398 Hayes St • Map F4 • (415) 551-1590 • Closed Mon • Dis. access • $$$

7 Fritz
Belgian frites and crêpes and a patio where Europhiles can smoke. ◎ 579 Hayes St • Map F4 • (415) 864-7654 • Dis. access • $

8 Powell's Place
Great soul food. The signature "Bar-B-Q" ribs are heavenly. ◎ 1521 Eddy St • Map F4 • (415) 409-1388 • $

9 Bia's Restaurant and Winebar
The top choice for Mediterranean cuisine. ◎ 1640 Haight St • Map E4 • (415) 861-8868 • Dis. access • $$

10 People's Café
For a cappuccino and a snack any time of day or night, this is a great hangout. ◎ 1419 Haight St • Map E4 • (415) 553-8842 • Dis. access • $

Left **Castro District bar** Right **View from Twin Peaks**

Southern Neighborhoods

THE SOUTHERN PART OF THE CITY *comprises some of the liveliest, most authentic parts of town – the clubs of SoMa, the gay world of the Castro, and the Latino Mission District. There are also some up-and-coming neighborhoods such as Bernal Heights and Glen Park, as the more central areas have priced creative types out toward the southern borders. Laid-back Noe Valley was the first such choice for high-rent refugees, but it, too, has gone gentrified and pushed people farther south.*

🔟 Sights and Neighborhoods

1 San Francisco Museum of Modern Art
2 Mission Dolores
3 Castro District
4 Twin Peaks
5 Noe Valley
6 Mission District
7 South of Market
8 Yerba Buena Center
9 China Basin
10 Potrero Hill

Noe Valley church

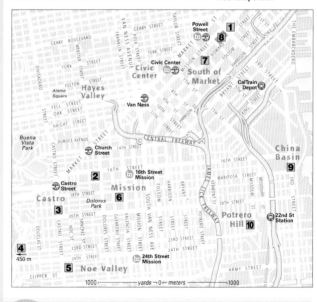

Statue of St Joseph, Mission Dolores

San Francisco Museum of Modern Art

San Francisco's home for its extensive modern art collection is as impressive outside as it is adaptable and awe-inspiring inside. Don't miss the top floors, featuring the latest digital installations, if you want to know what the cutting edge art world is honing itself on these days (see pp26–9).

Mission Dolores

The original Spanish Misión San Francisco de Asís, from which the city takes its name, is a marvel of preservation and atmospheric charm. It was founded in 1776, just a few weeks before the Declaration of Independence (see pp30–31).

Castro District

This hilly neighborhood around Castro Street is the center of San Francisco's high-profile gay community. The intersection of Castro and 18th streets is the self-proclaimed "Gayest Four Corners of the World," and this openly homosexual nexus emerged in the 1970s as the place of pilgrimage for gays and lesbians from all over the country and the world. Unlike other cities, where homosexuals once hid themselves away in dark corners of anonymous bars, the establishments here have full picture windows right on the street and are busy at all hours. Castro Street is closed off every Hallowe'en for the famous gay costume party that most agree is one of the city's best, second only perhaps to the Gay Pride Parade (see p75). Map E5

Twin Peaks

These two hills were first known in Spanish as *El Pecho de la Chola*, or "The Bosom of the Indian Girl." At the top, there is an area of parkland with steep and grassy slopes from which you can enjoy incomparable views of the whole of San Francisco. Twin Peaks Boulevard circles both hills near their summits, and there is plenty of parking near the viewing point. If you're up to the climb, take the footpath to the top, above the main viewing area, to get a 360-degree panorama. The residential districts on the slopes lower down have curving streets that follow the contours of the hills, rather than the formal grid pattern that predominates in most of the city (see p60). Map E6

Castro Theater, Castro District

Noe Valley

Once a simple working-class neighborhood, the 1970s brought hippies, gays, artists, and other Bohemian types to its slopes and it soon became an attractive alternative to other, more established quarters. In its heyday it was known as both "Nowhere Valley" for its relative remoteness, and as "Granola Valley" for its nature-loving denizens. Lately, it has been taken over by middle-class professionals, who value the area for its orderliness, but 24th Street still hums with activity and is lined with cafés, bookstores, and the occasional oddball shop. ✎ Map E6

Mission District

The teeming Hispanic world, with all the accompanying noise and confusion, constitutes the Mission, home to San Francisco's many Latinos. They have brought their culture with them – bustling *taquerias*, salsa clubs, Santeria shops, lively murals, and Spanish everywhere you look and listen. It's a loud, odoriferous place, with edgy crowds dodging each other along the main drags, Mission and Valencia streets and their connecting streets from Market to Cesar Chavez (Army). Its *folklórico* festivals are not to be missed, especially the Carnaval *(see p74)*. ✎ Map F5

A Gay City

After the free-love movement of the 1960s *(see p100)*, homosexuals realized that they, too, had rights to stand up for, and started moving into the Castro in the 1970s. In no time the neighborhood was a non-stop – and unstoppable – party of freewheeling sexual excess. Suddenly gays were "out" in legions, which brought with it political clout. Despite the AIDS plague, the city is still one of the easiest places in the world to live out an openly gay identity.

South of Market

The city's erstwhile rough-and-tumble warehouse district has been on the rise for the last few decades and continues to attract arty types as well as a whole range of clubs and cool cafés. Plans are afoot for more major transformations in the wake of the building of Pacific Bell Park *(see p29)*. ✎ Map R4

Yerba Buena Center

This area is fast becoming one of San Francisco's leading cultural centers for the performing arts, as well as a growing number of museums representing the city's ethnic diversity. Every year sees some new addition to the airy complex *(see pp28–9)*.

China Basin

This old shipping port has not been exempt from the upsurge of interest in the previously neglected industrial area. The main change has been wrought by the building of the new Pacific Bell Park, home to the city's major league

Mural, Mission District

SoMa Esplanade

baseball team, the San Francisco Giants, and developers have already put forth ideas of how the zone can be put to use. A number of restaurants, bars, and clubs, many with port views, have opened up here lately or have been refurbished and gentrified. ⌖ *Map H4*

Potrero Hill
At one time this usually sunny SoMa hill was set to become the next big thing. But somehow its isolation kept that from ever happening, cut off from the rest of the city, as it is, by freeways on three sides and its own precipitous inclines. Consequently, it has remained the quiet, pleasant neighborhood it always has been, with spectacular views. To be sure, a few more upmarket concerns are located here than before, and there are more restaurants and bars, but mostly it's thoroughly residential. However there are a few tourist sights that beckon here – the Anchor Brewing Company is worth the tour, and the Basic Brown Bear Factory is a hit with kids. ⌖ *Map H5 • Anchor Brewing Company: 1705 Mariposa St; Map H5 • (415) 863-8350 • Basic Brown Bear Factory: 2801 Leavenworth St, Floor 2; Map H5 • (866) 5BB-BEAR*

A Walk Around the Castro District

Begin at the city's gay mecca, the Church Street Muni Station on Upper Market. Decades ago, this corner developed a gay identity as the beginning point of the Castro neighborhood, but it is on the next block, between Sanchez and Noe, that the gay shops and venues really begin to proliferate.

The **Café Flore** (see p65) stands out as one of the premier gay hotspots for a drink, a meal, or just a gaze at the constant flow of fascinating clientele. Towards the corner of Castro is **The Cafe** at 2367 Market, offering a range of strong drinks accompanied by top 40 mixes to a trendy gay crowd.

Continuing on to Castro Street, take in Harvey Milk Plaza, with its huge rainbow flag, named after the slain gay leader (see p39). On the opposite corner, check out **Twin Peaks** (see p68) at 401 Castro, the oldest totally "out" gay bar, notable for its picture windows affording a full view of goings on, both inside and on the street.

Pushing on to No. 429, allow the Castro Theater to capture your attention, one of the city's most ornate cinema palaces, home to innumerable premieres of gay-themed films. Farther along at No. 489, **A Different Light Bookstore** (see p110) offers virtually every gay-themed book, magazine, and newspaper in the world.

Finally, just up 18th Street at No. 4121 is **Badlands** (see p69), a cruisy pickup scene that packs them in, especially after 10pm.

Left **Brand X Antiques** Right **Tibet Shop**

ᴛᴏᴘ10 Shops

Around Town – Southern Neighborhoods

1 Ed Hardy San Francisco

Without a doubt the premier antiques shop in town, featuring beautiful 18th- to 19th-century European masterworks, and Oriental pieces from as early as the Shang Dynasty (1500 BC). ✪ 188 Henry Adams St • Map G4 • (415) 626-6300

2 Jeremy's

A fabulous discount clothing boutique for men's and women's fashions, including Prada, Gucci, Armani, Ralph Lauren, DKNY, and more – all at reduced prices. ✪ 2 South Park • Map R6 • (415) 882-4929

3 A Different Light Bookstore

Probably the world's most complete gay and lesbian bookstore, from art and photography books to periodicals. ✪ 489 Castro St • Map E5 • (415) 431-0891

4 Brand X Antiques

The gay couple who own this shop have a discerning and humorous eye. In addition to baubles and furniture, the collection also features tongue-in-cheek vintage homoerotica. ✪ 570 Castro St • Map E5 • (415) 626-8908

5 Tibet Shop

In business for at least 40 years, it features a wide selection of merchandise from Tibet, Nepal, and Bhutan – clothing, jewelry, artifacts, art – at very reasonable prices. ✪ 4100 19th St at Castro • Map E5 • (415) 982-0326

6 Astrid's Rabat Shoes

If walking the steep city streets is challenging your footwear, this Noe Valley shop can fit you with a new pair of sturdy, stylish walking shoes. ✪ 3909 24th St • Map F6 • (415) 282-7400

7 Otsu

A boutique dedicated to providing high quality vegan products, such as shoes, belts, and bags, as well as books and paper products. ✪ 3253 16th St • Map F4 • (415) 255-7900, (866) HEYOTSU

8 Encantada Gallery

New shops open on lively Valencia Street almost monthly. This one specializes in Mexican folk art – Talavera pottery, textiles, religious icons, paper goods, and woodcarvings. ✪ 904–8 Valencia St • Map F5 • (415) 642-3939

9 Botanica Yoruba

The Santeria religion is the faith of many Latinos, and this shop caters to their ritualistic and spiritual needs. An array of potions and powders, candles and icons (see p45). ✪ 998 Valencia St • Map F5 • (415) 826-4967

10 Skechers

This vast store is a prime example of the discount emporiums up and down the Mission. If it's trendy running or walking shoes you're after, this is the place to find them. ✪ 2600 Mission St • Map F5 • (415) 401-6211

Left **Ten 15 Folsom** Right **Make-Out Room**

🔟 Nightclubs

1 Keur Baobab
West-African rhythms in the heart of the Mission. Senegalese decor, featuring masks and low tables, and cocktails made with fresh ginger and exotic juices. ◈ *3388 19th St • Map F5 • (415) 826-9287*

2 Make-Out Room
Cool live music provided by local up-and-comers and DJ nights make this a Mission favorite. The decor is original, the drinks are cheap, and the staff is appropriately witty. ◈ *3225 22nd St at Mission • Map F5 • (415) 647-2888*

3 Café
Something – and somebody – for everybody here at this camp, cruisy Castro old-timer that attracts gays, lesbians, and straights in equal doses. The outdoor balcony is great for people-watching. ◈ *2367 Market St at Castro • Map E5 • (415) 861-3846*

4 AsiaSF
Brazen Asian drag queens are your waitresses, who also perform bar-top numbers. The tropical cocktails glow in the dark. DJ disco-dancing downstairs. ◈ *201 9th St at Howard • Map G4 • (415) 255-2742*

5 The Endup
Formerly exclusively gay, as famously featured in *Tales of the City (see p52)*, this classic is now thoroughly mixed, featuring house music, and an all-day Sunday "T" Dance. ◈ *401 6th St at Harrison • Map R4 • (415) 357-0827*

6 The Stud Bar
Around for over 35 years, this formerly exclusive enclave of maleness is now popular with anybody who likes a rollicking lusty time. Theme nights include Trannyshack, a fabulous drag cabaret show. ◈ *399 9th St at Harrison • Map G4 • (415) 252-7883*

7 111 Minna Gallery
Art gallery by day and rave scene by night. Devotees call this the coolest place in town, with top DJs who mix everything from garage to world beat. ◈ *111 Minna St between New Montgomery & 2nd • Map P5 • (415) 462-0505*

8 El Rio
Different dance events every night of the week draw a diverse crowd ready to work their thing – Friday World Beat and Sunday Salsa Showcase are huge. ◈ *3158 Mission St • Map F5 • (415) 282-3325*

9 26 Mix
Located in deepest Mission District, this "sound lounge" is a cross between a large bar and a small nightclub. They offer a good mix of DJs and performers. ◈ *3024 Mission St at 26th St • Map F6 • (415) 826-7378*

10 Ten 15 Folsom
Perhaps the definitive SoMa club, with three levels of trance and techno spun by big-name DJs, complete with million-dollar light shows *(see p70)*. ◈ *1015 Folsom St at 6th • Map R4 • (415) 431-1200*

Left **The Bar on Castro** Right **Destino**

Bars and Clubs

1 Lucky 13
A chill-out punk bar where you can sport your new tattoo to an admiring audience. The jukebox is full of indie alternative sounds. ◊ *2140 Market St at Church • Map F4 • (415) 487-1313*

2 DNA Lounge
The recent return of this clubbers' favorite brings with it a juiced-up sound system, five bar areas, and a bigger dance floor. Webcasts of live concerts and DJ events, too. ◊ *375 11th St at Harrison • Map G4 • (415) 626-1409*

3 Destino
Traditional Spanish and South American music, with all the spirit that goes with it. Great drinks and Latino food, too *(see p67)*. ◊ *1815 Market St • Map F4 • (415) 552-4451*

4 The Bar on Castro
A friendly gay mix of young and old make this dark, very central bar one of the most popular on the street. It's only a bar – no food or music – and as such a great place to begin your evening's revelries. ◊ *456 Castro St • Map E5 • (415) 626-7220*

5 Azie
East meets West here, as the *feng shui* interior (tilted mirrors over the bar for watching your back), *sake* martinis, and "nine bites" nibbles would confirm. ◊ *826 Folsom St between 4th & 5th • Map R4 • (415) 538-0918*

6 Kate O'Brien's
SoMa Irish all the way, from Guinness to fish 'n' chips. The pub is large, the regulars relaxed and satisfied – it's a great place to kick back after a busy day. ◊ *579 Howard St between 1st & 2nd • Map P6 • (415) 882-7240*

7 The Knockout
A comfortable and stylish place with artwork, cool decor, and an attractive back bar. DJs and live music weekly. ◊ *3223 Mission St • Map F6 • (415) 550-6994*

8 Amber Bar and Cocktail Lounge
A place to mellow out on astrological cocktails, one specially concocted for each sign. It's the Age of Aquarius here, with the midnight blue and purple velvet decor, complete with starry galaxies. ◊ *718 14th St between Church & Sanchez • Map F4 • (415) 626-7827*

9 Rawhide II
Once catering to Country & Western loving males, it's now house music, but still pretty gay. The decor remains Wild West with a great patio. ◊ *280 7th St at Folsom • Map R3 • (415) 621-1197*

10 Lit
Proving there's something for everyone South of Market, the interior of this ornate cocktail lounge is replicated Victorian-era style. Music includes house and techno. ◊ *101 6th St at Mission • Map R3 • (415) 278-0940*

Price Categories

For a three-course meal for one with half a bottle of wine (or equivalent meal), taxes and extra charges.

$	under $20
$$	$20–$40
$$$	$40–$55
$$$$	$55–$80
$$$$$	over $80

Above **Pancho Villa Taqueria**

🔟 Places to Eat

1 Boulevard
The cuisine is mouth-watering Americana, but in very creative ways. The decor is *belle époque*; the service superior.
🕑 *1 Mission St at Steuart • Map H2 • (415) 543-6084 • Dis. access • $$$$*

2 Luna
A pleasant patio, and great food – try the grilled salmon salad with black-eyed peas. 🕑 *558 Castro St • Map E5 • (415) 621-2566 • $$*

3 Bagdad Café
This diner is all-American – buffalo wings, herb-roasted chicken, and pastries displayed in a revolving carousel. 🕑 *2295 Market St • Map F4 • (415) 621-4434 • Dis. access • $*

4 Sparky's Diner
Open 24 hours, this café is great for clubbers wanting to grab a late night breakfast. During the day it attracts families. 🕑 *242 Church St at Market • Map F4 • (415) 626-8666 • $*

5 Chow
Just off Market Street, Chow offers affordable pizzas, pastas, grilled and roasted meats, and a selection of beer and wine. Friendly service. 🕑 *215 Church St • Map F4 • (415) 552-2469 • Dis. access • $*

6 Pancho Villa Taqueria
Traditional Mexican fare here is prepared by jolly *muchachos* and *chiquitas*. 🕑 *3071 16th St • Map F4 • (415) 864-8840 • Dis. access • $*

7 La Rondalla
Kitsch and fun, this lively place serves Tex-Mex food until 3am. Wash it down with their potent margaritas. 🕑 *901–903 Valencia St at 20th • Map F5 • (415) 647-7474 • Closed Mon • No credit cards • Dis. access • $*

8 Caffè Centro
A brisk business in drinks, pastries, soups, and salads. Always crowded (*see p64*). 🕑 *102 South Park • Map R6 • (415) 882-1500 • Closed Sun • Dis. access • $*

9 Tita Hale 'Aina
This Hawaiian restaurant is complete with traditional music and tropical decor. Specialties include *kahlua* pig and *aku* tuna. 🕑 *3870 17th St at Market • Map F5 • (415) 626-2477 • Closed Mon • Dis. access • $*

10 Higher Ground Coffee House
A variety of sandwiches, omelets, and fresh salads, served with amazing homemade fries. 🕑 *691 Chenery St, Glen Park • (415) 587-2933 • No credit cards • Dis. access • $*

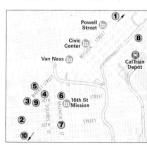

Note: Unless otherwise stated, all restaurants accept credit cards and serve vegetarian meals

Left **Legion of Honor** Right **Cliff House**

Oceanfront

A S WITH EVERY SEGMENT OF THIS CITY, *the area that faces the Pacific Ocean is a study in contrasts. Surprisingly to many, it contains terrains of natural beauty that are just as untamed and craggy as they always have been, particularly the rocky, windswept micro-climates that make up the cliffs and hidden ravines of Land's End. This has been the scene of innumerable shipwrecks throughout the city's history. Yet, just a few blocks away is Sea Cliff, one of the most exclusive residential neighborhoods in town. All up and down the area, beside blocks and blocks of tract homes, there are numerous parks and recreational possibilities, including, of course, surfing, if you're skilled and brave enough to face the unpredictable, freezing waters of the Pacific. Of all San Francisco's areas, this is the place where you're almost certain to encounter the city's infamous fog, but if the weather is clear there are great views of the offshore Seal Rocks and even the Farallon Islands. Further south, more activities can be enjoyed at Lake Merced.*

Koala, San Francisco Zoo

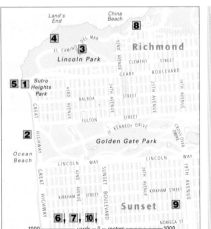

Sights

1. Cliff House
2. Ocean Beach
3. Legion of Honor
4. Oceanfront Parks
5. Seal Rocks
6. San Francisco Zoo
7. Sigmund Stern Grove
8. Sea Cliff
9. Sunset District
10. Lake Merced

Cliff House

Built in 1909, the present structure is the third on this site and was renovated in 2004. Its predecessor, a massively elaborate eight-story Victorian-Gothic castle that burned down in 1907, was built by the flamboyant entrepreneur Adolph Sutro (his estate overlooking Cliff House is now Sutro Heights Park). Cliff House has restaurants on the upper levels, observation decks overlooking the Pacific Ocean, a new wing containing two bars, a visitors' center, and the Camera Obscura. The Musée Méchanique has moved to Pier 45 at Fisherman's Wharf *(see p41)*. ✪ *Map A3 • Open 11am–7pm Mon–Fri, 10am–8pm Sat & Sun • Adm*

Ocean Beach

Most of San Francisco's western boundary is defined by this broad sweep of sand. Although sublime when viewed from Cliff House or Sutro Heights, the beach is dangerous for swimming due to its icy waters, rough shore breakers, and, most of all, rip currents that are powerful enough to drag even strong swimmers out to sea. Nevertheless, hardy surfers in thick wetsuits are a common sight, and in fine weather sunbathers and picnickers materialize. ✪ *The Great Hwy • Map A4*

Legion of Honor

The creation of Alma Bretteville Spreckels, heiress to the Spreckels sugar fortune, this museum is a replica of the Palais de la Légion d'Honneur in Paris. The original temporary structure was built for the 1915 Pan-Pacific Exposition to house French art, but Mrs Spreckels wanted to build a permanent version and employed the same architect

she commissioned to build her mansion in Pacific Heights *(see p99)*. It opened in 1924 and features a collection of medieval to 20th-century European art, with paintings by Monet, Rubens, and Rembrandt. Also excellent traveling exhibitions. ✪ *Lincoln Park, 34th Ave & Clement St • www.thinker.org • Map B3 • (415) 863-3330 • Open 9:30am–5pm Tue–Sun • Adm*

Oceanfront Parks

Lincoln Park, Land's End, and Sutro Heights Park are large green areas that overlook and hug the coast all along this northwestern corner of the peninsula. Stupendous Lincoln Park is the work of the indefatigable John McClaren *(see p21)*, and features coastal trails affording some of the best views of the Golden Gate Bridge. Land's End is a surprisingly rugged and wild stretch along the coastal cliffs that features a stony, picturesque cove, stretches of broad sand, and truly spectacular hiking. Gardens, statuary, and walls of the old Sutro estate still decorate Sutro Heights Park, dominating the entire coastal scene from its dramatic vantage point. ✪ *Map A3*

Land's End

Seal Rocks

5 Seal Rocks

The westernmost promontory on this tip of the peninsula is Point Lobos, the projection that forms Land's End's rocky cove. Along to the south from here down to Cliff House is a scattering of small, rocky islands frequented by seals – hence the name. Bring binoculars to spy on the seals and birds in their natural habitat. At night, from the beach or Cliff House promenade, the barking of the sea lions – like the keening of the foghorns – is both reassuring and eerie, and so very "San Francisco." On a clear day, 32 miles (50 km) off the coast, you can see the Farallon Islands, also inhabited by sea lions and with a state-protected rookery. ✍ Map A3

Cliff House and the Sutro Baths

Adolph Sutro came to San Francisco from Prussia in 1851, aged 21 and looking for gold. Instead, he became the Silver King of the Comstock Lode (Nevada), and brought his riches back to the city to invest them in land. His projects included building the first Cliff House, the popular Sutro Baths, and his own lavish estate. In the process, he transformed the Ocean Beach area into a recreational gem. The legacy lives on, despite the disappearance of all three of the famous buildings he constructed.

6 San Francisco Zoo

San Francisco Zoo is at the far southwest corner of the city, between the Pacific Ocean and Lake Merced. The complex is home to more than 1,000 species of birds, mammals, and insects, among which 20 are considered to be endangered – most notably the snow leopard, Bengal tiger, and jaguar. Gorilla World, Koala Crossing, and Children's Zoo are particular hits, as are the feeding times for the big cats (2pm at the Lion House Tue–Sun), penguins (3pm Fri–Wed and 2:30pm Thu at Penguin Island), and the Asian elephants (1:30pm daily). ✍ Sloat Blvd at Pacific Ocean • www.sfzoo.org • Buses 18 & 23 • Open 10am–5pm daily • (415) 753-7080 • Dis. access • Adm

7 Sigmund Stern Grove

This 63-acre ravine in the southern Sunset District is the site of the nation's original free summer arts festival, endowed in 1938 and still in operation. The Sunday programs may include classical music performed by the San Francisco Symphony Orchestra, opera, jazz, popular music, or productions by the San Francisco Ballet. The natural amphitheater is nestled within a fragrant eucalyptus and redwood grove. ✍ Sloat Blvd at 19th Ave, Sunset

8 Sea Cliff

Actor Robin Williams, a San Francisco native, has a home in this élite residential enclave, which stands in stark contrast to the natural coastal area all around it. Most of the luxurious homes are Mediterranean in style and date from the 1920s. Just below the neighborhood, China Beach – named after poor Chinese fishermen who used to camp here – is one of the safest beaches in the city for swimming and is equipped with showers and other facilities. Baker Beach, just to the north, is another popular beach *(see p76)*. ✤ *Map C2*

9 Sunset District

Like its counterpart, the Richmond District *(see p101)*, this neighborhood was part of the Outer Lands and is purely residential, consisting of row upon row of neat, look-alike houses. Yet, like the entire area along the ocean, this district is subject to a great deal of gray weather. Its one claim to fame is Sutro Tower, the pronged red-and-white television antenna that resembles something out of a science fiction movie. ✤ *Between Sloat Blvd & Golden Gate Park and Stanyan St & the Pacific Ocean • Map C5*

10 Lake Merced

Located at the beginning of scenic Skyline Boulevard, this attractive lake, set amid verdant hills, extends across the southern end of the Sunset District. Relatively undeveloped and certainly under-used, it nevertheless gets its share of recreation enthusiasts. They come for the municipal Harding Park 18-hole Golf Course, and the biking and running trails that circle the lake's green shoreline. ✤ *Hwy 35*

Sunset District

A Two-Hour Hike Around Land's End

This section of the coast is amazingly wild, especially considering that it is actually within the city limits. Note that portions of the hike are very rugged, so dress accordingly, with good footwear.

Begin at the far end of the Merrie Way parking lot and take the steps down. Follow the trail that passes by the **Sutro Baths** ruins *(see p39)*, to your left as you descend. Continue on along to the Overlook, from which you can take in **Seal Rocks** and much of the Pacific panorama.

Now double back a bit to pick up the trail that continues along the coast. You will see the remains of concrete military bunkers, which have been broken and tilted by the unstable land, and now decorated with graffiti. Soon you come to a beach below rocky cliffs; note that the surging water is very unpredictable here, so be very attentive. Continue walking and you will arrive at Land's End Cove, where a makeshift beach, using rock walls as windbreakers, is popular with nudists.

Next, climb up one of the sets of wooden steps to join the path up above and continue on around the bend, where you will be greeted with a stunning view of the **Golden Gate Bridge** *(see pp8–9)*. Keep going all the way to Eagle's Point and return by way of the higher trail that winds through **Lincoln Park** *(see p73)*.

For a meal after your hike visit **Cliff House** *(see p121)*.

Following pages: **Cliff House and the Pacific Ocean**

117

Left **Williams-Sonoma** Right **Aquaholics**

TOP10 Shops

1 Troika
With the atmosphere of a pawnshop and the thick sound of Russian being spoken, this shop reflects the émigré neighborhood in which it's located. All sorts of collectibles and gift ideas, mostly of Russian origin. ✆ *6300 Geary Blvd • Map C3 • (415) 387-4141*

2 Old Stuff
One of several antiques shops along this strip of Clement, this one has everything, from furniture to jewelry, to lamps, to glass and china. ✆ *2325 Clement St • Map C3 • (415) 668-2220*

3 Gaslight & Shadows Antiques
The specialty here is porcelain, specifically the precious, delicate masterpieces turned out by the various makers in the town of Limoges, France. It's like visiting a museum dedicated to this fine artform. Dolls, costume jewelry, and Oriental rugs, too. ✆ *2335 Clement St • Map C3 • (415) 387-0633*

4 The Garden Spot
Besides some very fine chests, chairs, bureaus, and the like, treasures of all sorts are tucked away here. ✆ *3029 Clement St • Map B3 • (415) 751-8190*

5 Aquaholics
Every sort of surf gear, including the extra-thick wetsuits you need to survive these northern waters. ✆ *2830 Sloat Blvd between 46th & 47th avenues • (415) 242-9283*

6 Stonestown Galleria
Upmarket Nordstrom and all-purpose Macy's are the anchor stores to this traditional indoor-outdoor shopping center. It isn't much different from shopping centers all over America, but you might find prices cheaper here than in other parts of the city. ✆ *19th Ave & Winston Drive*

7 Borders Books & Music
This chain bookstore offers a good selection of the latest titles, some excellent bargain choices, and a snack bar. ✆ *233 Winston Drive • (415) 731-0665*

8 Williams-Sonoma
The renowned kitchen, cookware, and serving-ware dealer originated in Northern California. Products from around the world, chosen for functionality and beauty. ✆ *3251 20th Ave, Stonestown Galleria • (415) 242-1473*

9 Ann Taylor
Simplicity and comfortable fit are the keynotes of the women's clothing designed by Ann Taylor. Elegant suits, luxurious silk sweaters, linen casuals, or sporty khakis. ✆ *3251 20th Ave, Stonestown Galleria • (415) 564-0229*

10 Bailey Banks & Biddle
The finest gems are set off by elegant designs created by this jeweler, in business since 1832. They also have Lladró figurines. ✆ *3251 20th Ave, Stonestown Galleria • (415) 759-5310*

Price Categories

For a three-course meal for one with half a bottle of wine (or equivalent meal), taxes and extra charges.

$	under $20
$$	$20–$40
$$$	$40–$55
$$$$	$55–$80
$$$$$	over $80

Above **Beach Chalet Brewery**

🔟 Places to Eat

1 Cliff House
Standard American fare, but the real reason to come here is to see the Pacific crashing on the cliffs below and to witness the wonderful sunsets (see p115). ◎ 1090 Point Lobos Ave • Map A3 • (415) 386-3330 • Dis. access • $$

2 Beach Chalet Brewery
Again, you come for the view, both outside, of the ocean, and inside, of the murals. The food is not much to write home about. ◎ 1000 Great Hwy • Map A4 • (415) 386-8439 • Dis. access • $$$

3 Louis'
Diner food with wonderful views of Seal Rock and Land's End. Every American favorite you can name. ◎ 902 Point Lobos Ave • Map A3 • (415) 387-6330 • Dis. access • $$

4 Ton Kiang
Many say this place has the best dim sum in the city. Always fresh, hot, and tasty, with various specialties. ◎ 5821 Geary Blvd • Map C3 • (415) 387-8273 • Dis. access • $$

5 Chapeau!
Perhaps the most authentic French bistro, run by a talented husband and wife team. He's the sommelier and knows how to assign the treasures from his list. Service is refined, and every bite memorable. ◎ 1408 Clement St at 15th Ave • Map C3 • (415) 750-9787 • Closed Mon • Dis. access • $$$$$

6 Kabuto Sushi
A great Japanese restaurant – the sashimi melts in the mouth. ◎ 5116 Geary Blvd at 15th Ave • Map C3 • (415) 752-5652 • Closed Mon & Sun • Dis. access • $$

7 Pizzetta
Thin and crisp pizza topped with organic ingredients. ◎ 211 23rd Ave • Map C3 • (415) 379-9880 • Closed Mon L & Tue • No credit cards • Dis. access • $

8 Thanh Long
Fine Vietnamese food – try garlic noodles or roasted crab. ◎ 4101 Judah St at 46th Ave • Map A5 • (415) 665-1146 • Dis. access • $$

9 Java Beach Café
This cozy café serves sandwiches, soup, and pastries in a nautical-themed interior. ◎ 1396 Judah St • Map A5 • (415) 665-5282 • $

10 Chevy's
Fresh Tex-Mex in generous portions. The chips and salsa are free. ◎ 3251 20th Ave • (415) 665-8705 • Dis. access • $

Note: Unless otherwise stated, all restaurants accept credit cards and serve vegetarian meals

Left **Mormon Temple, Oakland** Right **Point Bonita lighthouse, Marin County Headlands**

The Bay Area

IN LOCAL PARLANCE, THE BAY AREA *breaks down into The City, the East Bay, Marin, the Peninsula, and the South Bay. Although technically Santa Clara and San Jose – and certainly Santa Cruz and Capitola – do not touch the waters of the Bay, psychologically they still embody the same liberal, open-minded ethos that so defines this area. This is probably because the dominant mentality of this swatch of Northern California is so definably different from those of Southern California and the Central Valley. In towns such as Berkeley, Mill Valley, and Stanford the emphasis is on progressive thinking; smaller enclaves such as Bolinas are determined to live life in harmony with the breathtaking nature all around them.*

Sather Tower, Berkeley campus

🔟 Sights

1. Berkeley
2. Oakland
3. Marin County Headlands
4. Sausalito
5. Mill Valley
6. Mount Tamalpais
7. Stinson Beach
8. Bolinas
9. Palo Alto & Stanford
10. Tiburon

Wellman Hall, University of California, Berkeley

1 Berkeley

Its days as "Berzerkly," when student protesters and tear-gas clouds filled the streets in the 1960s, are only a fading memory now, although Telegraph Avenue still keeps some of the counter-cultural traditions alive. A great university, "Cal's" faculty boasts some dozen Nobel Laureates, while beautiful parks, tree-lined streets, and unique shops typify this East Bay enclave. Berkeley continues to give more "power to the people" than any other US city, with a host of public services and aid to the disadvantaged that puts other communities to shame. ◈ BART Berkeley

2 Oakland

Gertrude Stein's famous dictum about her home town, that "there is no there there," is being challenged these days by a very proactive new mayor, Jerry Brown (see p39). Oakland's image, notorious for racial unrest and crime in the past, is being cleaned up to present a more visitor-friendly face, and there has been an influx of creative types who have moved here to flee the high rents of San Francisco. Oakland's attractions include huge Lake Merritt, which offers a range of recreational possibilities, a beautiful Mormon temple and its Museum of California (see p126). ◈ BART 12th St

3 Marin County Headlands

To visit these raw, wild hills with aston-ishingly beautiful views is to enter another world; yet it's only half an hour's drive away, by way of the Golden Gate Bridge. The scale of the rolling terrain is immense, and the precipitous drops into the ocean dramatic. This is an unspoiled area of windswept ridges, sheltered valleys, and deserted beaches (see p76). ◈ Muni Bus 76

4 Sausalito

A former fishing community and now an upscale commuter area and tourist haven, this small town offers spectacular views of the city from its Bridgeway Avenue promenade. Historically, it has been an artists' town, with an eccentric mix of residents (see p54). Bungalows cling to the hillsides and boats fill the picturesque marinas, many of them houseboats that locals live in year-round. Excellent restaurants, accommodations, and some unique shopping possibilities, too. ◈ US 101

Marina, Sausalito

From Sausalito, the Call of the Sea is a tall-ship that sails out on the Bay, with buffet served. Telephone (415) 331-3214 for details.

Around Town – The Bay Area

Great Bay Area Universities

Palo Alto's Stanford University is the Bay Area's most famous private institution of higher learning, inaugurated in 1891. However, in terms of intellectual clout, the University of California at Berkeley, the oldest campus in the California system, stands shoulder to shoulder, considering the number of Nobel Laureates on the faculty and its international importance. Stanford is known for business, law, and medicine, Berkeley for law, engineering, and nuclear physics. Both universities are among the most selective in the country.

Mill Valley

5 Home to a well-known film festival, but perhaps more famous as the quintessential Marin hometown. It's wealthy, relaxed, and beautiful, and the well-educated populace is given to progressively liberal views on just about every topic. The old part of town is flanked by wonderful stands of redwoods, lined with old buildings that house restaurants and unusual shops, and the whole centers around an eternally pleasant public square where people come to hang out. ✪ Off Hwy 101

Mount Tamalpais

6 No more breathtaking view exists than that from the summit of mystic "Mount Tam," sacred to the Native Americans who once lived here. At 2,570 ft (785-m) high, those who hike up to the summit can take in practically the entire Bay Area at a glance. The area all around is a state park, a wilderness nature preserve with more than 200 miles (320 km) of trails that wind through redwood groves and alongside creeks. There are picnic areas, campsites, and

Greek Theater, Mount Tamalpais

meadows for kite flying. The steep, rough tracks here gave rise to the invention of the mountain bike. ✪ Hwy 1

Stinson Beach

7 Since the early days of the 20th century, this has been a popular vacation spot; the first visitors came on ferries from San Francisco and were met by horse-drawn carriages. Stinson remains the preferred swimming beach for the whole area (see p76), and nearby Seadrift is an upscale community of second or third homes of the wealthy. The stretch of soft sand here and the spectacular sunsets set off the quaint village, with its good restaurants and interesting shops. You can reach it via the coast route, but the drive up and over Highway 1 provides the most dramatic arrival, affording inspiring views as you exit the forest onto the bare headlands. ✪ Hwy 1

Bolinas

8 The next community up from Stinson is a hippie artists' village that time forgot. Intensely private, the citizens regularly take down all road signs indicating the way to their special place to keep visitors from finding them. Potters and other craftspeople sell their wares in the funky gallery, organic produce and vegetarians are the rule, and 1960s idealism still predominates. 🔊 Hwy 1

9 Palo Alto and Stanford

An erstwhile sleepy university town, Palo Alto has most recently experienced a boom as the hub of Silicon Valley, and driving force of the "New Economy." Although a lot of the gilding has lately fallen off the lily, this town has been left with a considerably dressed-up appearance, as well as many fancy restaurants, hotels, and shops. The town is home to prestigious Stanford University, with its beautiful, well-tended campus (see p79). 🔊 Hwys 101 & 82

10 Tiburon

Possibly Marin County's smartest community, it stands as a less hectic alternative to Sausalito for its views and restaurants. Here, 100-year-old houseboats ("arks") have been pulled ashore, lined up, and refurbished, forming what is called "Ark Row," where you'll find shops and restaurants that enhance the charm of this waterfront village. Tiburon also offers scenic parks along the shore, facing Angel Island and the city. 🔊 Hwy 131

Tiburon

A Morning Walk Around Berkeley

🕐 Begin at the University Visitor Center on Oxford St at the end of University Avenue, where you can pick up information and maps. Follow around to University Drive and on to the university campus, passing Romanesque Wellman Hall, then take a left on Cross Campus Road. Straight ahead is the main campus landmark, the 307-ft (94-m) Sather Tower, also known simply as the Campanile, based on the famous belltower in Venice's Piazza San Marco.

Now continue on to rejoin University Drive and go around to the Hearst Greek Theater, venue for excellent concerts of all sorts. Next, head for handsome Sather Gate, which leads into Sproul Plaza, epicenter of the student Free Speech Movement protests that erupted into almost non-stop socio-political unrest in the 1960s and 1970s.

Exit the campus onto Telegraph Avenue, a kind of Haight-Ashbury East-Bay with radical vibes all its own. Cody's, at the corner of Haste Street, is Berkeley's most famous bookstore, and one block over is idealistic People's Park. Continue on back to Bancroft Way to pay a visit to the excellent University Art Museum and the Pacific Film Archive.

🍴 After your walk, for lunch try the unique Blue Nile, (2525 Telegraph Ave at Dwight Way • (510) 540-6777 • Dis. access • $$). It offers Ethiopian family-style dining, with delicious stews and homemade honey wine.

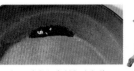

Left **Octopus, California Ecosystems** Centre & Right **Gold Rush Artifacts**

TOP 10 Oakland Museum of CA Features

1 The Building
The museum building is an outstanding example of modern design. Opened in 1969, it is composed of reinforced concrete and consists of three levels of tiered terraces. To soften the angularity, roof gardens have been planted, accented with sculpture.

2 California Ecosystems
The Natural Science Gallery is located on the first level. It features "A Walk Across California," including a diorama of a Sacramento delta marsh showing fish, bird, and insect life, and another of a mountain lion and its prey, demonstrating nature's food chain.

3 The Earliest Californians
The Cowell Hall of California History on the second level traces early human history in the state, documented by basketry, stone tools, clothing, and rituals.

4 Mission-era Artifacts
An 18th-century icon of St Jerome is just one remnant of the Spanish Mission years. You'll also find early colonial tools, and a section of adobe wall.

5 Gold Rush Artifacts
"Immigrants and Settlers" and "Adventurers and Gold-seekers" chronicle the lives of those who came to California from all over the world in the 19th century, hoping to strike it rich. You'll see gold prospecting tools.

6 Earthquake Artifacts
A collection of objects that pertain to the 1906 earthquake are on display here, including porcelain cups and saucers fused by the heat of the fire that destroyed so much of the city.

7 Dream on Wheels
"Seekers, Innovators and Achievers" celebrates the "California Dream," in which the automobile played so large a part in the postwar boom. A drive-in restaurant sign, jukebox, and gleaming hot-rod capture the feel of the 1950s.

8 Art Gallery
The third level is devoted to the Gallery of California Art, featuring works by artists who have studied, lived, and worked here. Included are works by 19th-century landscape painters, California Impressionists, members of the Bay Area Figurative movement, and later works by the likes of David Ireland.

9 Photography Gallery
The Gallery of California Art also has a fine collection of the work of California photographers, including Ansel Adams, Edward Weston, and Dorothea Large.

10 California Crafts
The largest collection of decorative work, including murals and furniture, by California Arts and Crafts practitioners Arthur and Lucia Kleinhaus Mathews.

Oakland Museum of California, 1000 Oak St, is open 10am–5pm Wed–Sat, noon–5pm Sun. Website: www.museumca.org

Left **Roller Coaster, Santa Cruz** Right **Santa Cruz coastline**

TOP10 Best of the Rest

1 San Rafael
Located in the heart of Marin County, this town has a charming historic center loaded with good restaurants and shops. When the street market takes over the main drag every Thursday evening, it's transformed into an impromptu pleasure fair. ⊗ *Hwy 101*

2 Belvedere Island
This garden island, attached by a causeway to Tiburon, is one of the most exclusive residential areas in the Bay. It's worth a visit to take in the palatial homes and their sumptuous settings.

3 Point Reyes
This wild and windswept peninsula is a huge haven for wildlife, including a herd of tule elk, birds, and wildflowers. The area is also home to cattle and dairy ranches. You can watch migrating whales offshore from December to mid-March. ⊗ *Hwy 1 to Olema, then signposted to Point Reyes*

4 San Gregorio and Pescadero
San Gregorio, protected by cliffs, is the Bay Area's oldest nudist beach. Pescadero, in addition to having a state beach with wonderful tidepools, is also a lovely town that looks like something out of the Old West, complete with a whitewashed wooden church. The thriving farming community produces asparagus and pumpkins. ⊗ *Hwy 1*

5 Woodside
This bucolic residential area is home to many of the Bay Area's first families, who built fabulous mansions here in the late 19th century. ⊗ *Hwy 280*

6 La Honda
The most picturesque way to make the approach to the tiny community of La Honda and the Skyline Boulevard *(see p60)* is Old La Honda Road. ⊗ *Hwy 280*

7 Los Gatos & Saratoga
These outpost towns still retain some frontier atmosphere, although they are now communities for the movers and shakers of Silicon Valley. ⊗ *Hwy 280*

8 San Jose
This sprawling town is an integral part of Silicon Valley enterprises and has popular attractions. ⊗ *Map Hwy 101*

9 Winchester Mystery House
The eccentric 19th-century home of the rifle heiress, Sarah Winchester, took 38 years to build and includes stairways leading to nowhere and windows set into floors. ⊗ *525 S Winchester Blvd, San Jose • Open 9am–8pm daily • Adm*

10 Santa Cruz & Capitola
This area offers some of the Bay's best swimming. Santa Cruz also features the famous Boardwalk, a vintage amusement park. ⊗ *Hwy 1*

Left **Via Diva** Right **Greenwood**

Bay Area Shops

1 Stanford Shopping Center

One of the first shopping centers in the Bay Area, it has been catering to the needs of pampered Stanford students for some 50 years. The shops and eateries are in keeping with the university's exclusive status. ⊗ *180 El Camino Real, Palo Alto • Hwy 101 • (650) 617-8200*

2 Sweet Dreams

An old-fashioned candy shop, with jars and jars of all the traditional treats, plus some innovative confections. Adjoining is a charming toyshop, too, as well as Teddy's Little Closet kids' clothing. ⊗ *2901 College Ave, Berkeley • Hwy 80 • (510) 549-1211*

3 Gene Hiller

For over 50 years, this exclusive menswear store has been offering the finest imported designer clothing – including Brioni, Zegna, and Canali – from classic formal to casual. ⊗ *729 Bridgeway Ave, Sausalito • Hwy 101*

4 Claudia Chapline Gallery and Sculpture Garden

In a great setting near the beach, the Chapline sculpture garden is full of delights, especially the brilliant kinetic pieces driven by the wind, which are the work of Lyman Whitaker. Inside, the variety and quality of painted and mixed-media work is very compelling. ⊗ *3445 Shoreline Hwy, Stinson Beach • Hwy 1 • (415) 868-2308*

5 Via Diva

This collection of art and artifacts includes treasures from China, Indonesia, India, Thailand, and South America. ⊗ *516 Irwin San Rafael • Off Hwy 101 • (415) 257-8881*

6 What the Traveller Saw

Highlights upscale world art. Balinese wood carvings, silk ties, blankets, weavings, fountains, and much more. ⊗ *1880 Salano Ave, Berkeley • Hwy 880 • (510) 527-1775*

7 Greenwood

Marin's finest shop for one-of-a-kind handcrafted items made by local, regional, national, and international artisans. ⊗ *32B Miller Ave, Mill Valley • Off Hwy 101 • (415) 389-5037*

8 Paul & Shark

An Italian haberdashery for the yachting set. Elegant clothing for men and women. ⊗ *22 El Portal, Sausalito • Hwy 101 • (415) 331-0588*

9 Shady Lane

The undertaking of a collective of artists who wanted to create a showcase for their work. It's the perfect place to find a special gift. ⊗ *441 University Ave, Palo Alto • Hwy 101 • (650) 321-1099*

10 Global Exchange

Beautiful handmade creations from Vietnam, Indonesia, Mexico, and Senegal. The producers receive most of the profits. ⊗ *2840 College Ave, Berkeley • Hwy 80 • (510) 548-0370*

Above **Piazza d'Angelo**

Price Categories

For a three-course meal for one with half a bottle of wine (or equivalent meal), taxes and extra charges.	
$	under $20
$$	$20–$40
$$$	$40–$55
$$$$	$55–$80
$$$$$	over $80

⏃ Places to Eat

1 The Lark Creek Inn
The redwood-shaded garden loveliness of this Marin hideaway is impossible to fault. The food is innovative New American cuisine such as roasted parsnip soup with black truffles (see p63). ❧ 234 Magnolia Ave, Larkspur • Hwy 101 • (415) 924-7766 • Dis. access • $$$

2 Piazza d'Angelo
This first-rate Italian has a creative menu and a fine selection of wines. Indoor and outdoor seating, a lavish dessert cart, and a very happening feel. ❧ 22 Miller Ave, Mill Valley • Off Hwy 101 • (415) 388-2000 • Dis. access • $$

3 Las Camelias
Everything here is home-made and unusual. The decor is particularly appealing, most of the art being the work of the charming hostess-owner. ❧ 912 Lincoln Ave, San Rafael • Hwy 101 • (415) 453-5850 • Dis. access • $$

4 The Bridgeway Café
Great for breakfast or lunch; you'll find a range of American favorites at this cozy little diner looking right out onto the Bay. ❧ 633 Bridgeway, Sausalito • Hwy 101 • (415) 332-3426 • Dis. access • $

5 Parkside
Creative American brunch at picnic tables on the patio, or in the dining room. Try the barbecued glazed salmon with wild rice. ❧ 43 Arenal Ave, Stinson Beach • Hwy 1 • (415) 868-1272 • Dis. access • $$

6 Chez Panisse
A very popular Berkeley spot which has been serving up excellent California cuisine since 1971. The upstairs cafe offers a cheaper alternative. ❧ 1517 Shattuck Ave, Berkeley • Hwy 80 • (510) 548-5525 • Closed Sun • $$$

7 Café Eritrea d'Afrique
An acclaimed restaurant serving Eritrean and Ethiopean cuisine in a relaxing and friendly atmosphere. They offer an all-you-can-eat veggie buffet on Wednesdays and Fridays. ❧ 4096 Telegraph Ave, Oakland • Hwy 880 • (510) 547-4520 • $

8 Amber India
Northern Indian recipes, freshly prepared so that the full flavors of the ingredients come through. ❧ 2290 El Camino Real, Mountain View • (650) 968-7511 • Dis. access • $$

9 Los Gatos Coffee Roasting Company
Sit here and watch the busy street, lined with antiques stores, sip your choice of delicious brew, and snack on tempting tidbits. ❧ 101 West Main St, Los Gatos • Hwy 280 • (408) 354-3263 • Dis. access • $

10 Gayle's
This bakery and rosticceria has an extraordinary selection of gourmet treats – try the cappuccino cake. ❧ 504 Bay Ave, Capitola • Hwy 1 • (831) 462-1200 • Dis. access • $

Note: Unless otherwise stated, all restaurants accept credit cards and serve vegetarian meals

STREETSMART

SAN FRANCISCO'S TOP 10

Left **San Francisco Visitor Information Center** Right **Outdoor dining in the fall**

Planning Your Trip

1 Tourist Offices
Plenty of websites, representing the principal tourist agencies, tell you how to tackle the practical aspects of organizing a visit to San Francisco. Or they will send you materials by standard mail *(see box)*.

2 Media
The city's daily and weekly newspapers – the weekly ones are free and super-abundant – are loaded with information about all the things going on in town. Perusing their websites will give you a head start on planning your trip. ✎ *San Francisco Chronicle (daily): www.sfgate.com • San Francisco Bay Guardian (weekly): www.sfbg.com • SF Weekly: ww.sfweekly.com • Bay Area Reporter (gay): www.ebar.com • San Francisco Frontiers (gay): www.frontiersweb.com*

3 Internet
Any search for places, people, or events to do with San Francisco will turn up a plethora of finds, but two sites give a good overview and guidance. These are: www.sanfranciscocitysearch.com and www.baycityguide.com

4 Maps
San Francisco is very easy to find your way around, but study the general layout in advance. Free maps are available from tourist offices.

5 Visas
Canadian citizens need only proof of citizenship. Most European citizens, as well as Japanese and a few others, need only a valid passport and a non-refundable return ticket originating outside the US to qualify for a 90-day visa. Other nationalities must secure a visa, before traveling, from a US consulate or embassy.

6 Insurance
Buy a good travel insurance policy to cover lost baggage, canceled flights, and minor medical bills. And, since the US generally does not have public healthcare, international health coverage is the wisest way to go. Save all receipts.

7 US Embassies and Consulates
US diplomatic missions are found in virtually every country's capital. They will be able to provide you with information about San Francisco, as well as answer any questions you may have about visa requirements. ✎ *Australia: www.dfat.gov.au/missions • Canada: www.usembassycanada.gov • France: www.amb-usa.fr • Germany: www.usembassy.de • Ireland: http://dublin.usembassy.gov/ • New Zealand: http://wellington.usembassy.gov • UK: www.usembassy.org.uk*

8 When to Go
The nicest months are September and October. The summer is best to avoid, as coastal areas and the city tend to be blanketed in fog and points inland are blazing hot and dusty.

9 What to Take
Generally, San Franciscans dress casually. The best rule of thumb is to travel with as little as possible – if you're missing something, you can buy it.

10 How Long to Stay
Unless you are very unusual, you will fall in love with this city and want to stay as long as possible. A week should allow you to take in all the major sights; two weeks will leave enough time to explore the coast and the Wine Country.

Tourist Offices

San Francisco Convention and Visitors Bureau
201 3rd St, CA 94107
• (415) 974-6900
• www.sfvisitor.org

San Francisco Visitors Information Center
900 Market St • Map Q4 • (415) 391-2000

California Welcome Center
Pier 39, 2nd level
• (415) 956-3493
• www.visitcwc.com

If you want to try one of the top restaurants or attend one of the most popular shows, make a reservation before you leave home.

Left **Greyhound bus** Right **Amtrak train**

Getting to San Francisco

1 San Francisco International Airport

Fifteen miles (24 km) south of the city and linked by two freeways and a host of inexpensive public transport options and private shuttles, as well as taxis and limos, SFO is very conveniently located and efficiently run. The airport has three terminals, and the largest international terminal in the US. Information booths are located downstairs and are open from 8am to 1:30am.
- *SFO: (650) 876-7809*
- *www.flysfo.com*

2 Oakland International Airport

The East Bay's major airport is only a bit farther away from the city, so it can be a handy alternative. One advantage is fewer crowds. Again, there is a choice of transport to get you back and forth. *Oakland International Airport: (510) 577-4000*
- *www.oaklandairport.com*

3 San Jose International Airport

If your destination is more Silicon Valley than San Francisco, you've come to the right airport. It's 50 miles (80 km) south of the city but only 20 miles (32 km) south of Palo Alto. *San Jose International Airport: (408) 277-4759* • *www.sjc.org*

4 Customs

You're allowed to bring in 1 liter of liquor and 200 cigarettes duty-free, and $100 worth of gifts. If you're carrying more than $10,000 in anything negotiable, you must declare the excess.

5 Left Luggage

SF International has lockers in all boarding areas that you can secure for up to 24 hours. For anything bigger or that you want to store for a longer time, go to the Luggage Storage in the upper-level passageway between the South and International Terminals.

6 Lost Property

Each airport has a Lost Property service. If you leave something on public transport, there are numbers for each system, and taxi companies will also try to locate your possessions.
- *SF Property Control: 850 Bryant St; (415) 553-1377*
- *Muni (415) 923-6164*
- *BART (510) 464-7090*

7 Greyhound

There are 12 buses every 24 hours from Los Angeles to San Francisco and vice versa. It takes 8–12 hours but is the cheapest option. Greyhounds also go all over the US, but, although low in dollars, you pay in time, and discomfort.
- *Transbay Terminal • 425 Mission St • (415) 495-1575*
- *www.greyhound.com*

8 Amtrak

The main Bay Area terminal for the US national railway system is in Oakland, offering a free shuttle bus to the city, stopping at the CalTrain station in the South of Market district and at the Ferry Building. The Coast Starlight route runs from Seattle down to Los Angeles daily, and vice versa.
- *Amtrak: 1-800-872-7245*
- *www.amtrak.com*

9 Shuttles

One of the best ways to get from and to the airport is to use the shuttle services, some of which are door-to-door. You can pick them up on the upper level at SFO. When making the return trip, however, you'll need to book the door-to-door type. Others leave regularly from major hotels and pick-up spots.
- *SFO Airporter: (415) 558-8500; www.supershuttle. com • Bayporter Express: 1-877-467-1800 or (415) 467-1800; www.bayporter.com*

10 Taxis and Limousines

Taxis can be taken from the lower level of SFO, and a typical journey into the city will cost roughly $40, plus a standard 10 percent tip. Limousines are more costly and you will have to book in advance. *Pure Luxury Limousines: (415) 485-1764; www.pureluxury.com*

Left **Cycling in Golden Gate Park** Right **Bay Area ferry**

Getting Around San Francisco

1 Cable Cars
Pure tourism, of course, but also one of the most enjoyable ways of getting around Downtown and Fisherman's Wharf. Pricey at $5 per ride, it becomes a bargain if you buy the CityPass ($39.95), which also gets you into many sights and is good for unlimited travel on the Muni transport system for a week from the time of first use. The Muni Passport can be used on the entire Muni system including cable cars.

2 Streetcars
The Muni Metro trams mostly run under Market Street and then make their way into the western neighborhoods. One line, the F, consists of vintage streetcars from around the world that decoratively traverse the Market Street circuit above ground.

3 Buses
To use Muni, you can either get the CityPass, or you can purchase Muni Passports for varying terms (1 day, 3 days, 7 days, or a full month). The bus system is simple to use and will get you around this compact metropolis in good time, though rarely on schedule. Many bus stops have local bus route maps, as well as maps of the system as a whole. ✆ (415) 673-6864 • www.sfmuni.com

4 BART
The Bay Area Rapid Transit system (BART) serves a large arc of San Francisco and connects it very efficiently with the East Bay. There are also plans to extend it to San Francisco International Airport (see p133). BART stations are underground and many are shared with Muni Metro stops. ✆ (415) 989-2278 • www.bart.gov

5 CalTrain
Since Peninsula residents voted against extending BART down south, this commuter train provides the most efficient public service to places such as Palo Alto and Stanford University (see p125). It is comfortable, punctual, and cheap. ✆ CalTrain Terminal: 4th St between Townsend & King • 1-800-660-4287 • www.caltrain.com

6 Ferries
The ferries provide wonderful, inexpensive excursions to many picturesque points. The Blue & Gold Fleet serves Alcatraz, Angel Island, and Sausalito from Pier 41, the East Bay and Tiburon from the Ferry Building. Golden Gate Transit serves Sausalito and Larkspur from the Ferry Building. ✆ Blue & Gold Fleet: (415) 773-1188; www.blueandgoldfleet.com • Golden Gate Transit Ferry Service: (415) 923-2000; www.goldengate.org

7 Taxis
Due to a very tight licensing system, San Francisco does not have enough taxis, despite the poor car-to-parking-spot ratio. You can usually snag one by lining up at a major hotel.

8 Car
Rent a car only if you want to head outside the city. Driving here can be challenging to the uninitiated, and it isn't necessary for getting around, given the decent public transportation. ✆ American Automobile Association: 150 Van Ness Ave; (415) 565-2711

9 Motorbike
Zipping up and down San Francisco's hills on a motorcycle or scooter can be great fun. It's also a fast, efficient way to get around town. The same driving and parking rules apply to motorbikes as to cars. ✆ Dubbelju Motorcycle Rentals: 271 Clara St, between 5th & 6th • (415) 495-2774 • www.dubbelju.com

10 Bicycle
Scenic routes have been designated. It's a great, healthy way to take in the wonderful sights and parks, and convenient given the city's small size. ✆ Bicycle Information Line: (415) 585-2453 • Blazing Saddles: Fisherman's Wharf; (415) 202-8888; www.blazingsaddles.com

Organized tours of the city, Muir Woods, the Wine Country, and Monterey cost from $42. Telephone (415) 434-8687 for details.

Left **Parking instruction sign** Right **Waiting staff should be tipped**

Things to Avoid

1 Don't Call it "Frisco"
Either say it all – "San Francisco" – or call it simply "The City." It's the name of a saint, after all, of whom San Franciscans are every bit as proud as they are of their city.

2 Driving Challenges
When you parallel park pointing up the hill, turn your wheels toward the center of the street; when pointing downhill, turn your wheels toward the sidewalk. That's the way to prevent runaway cars. If you are driving a manual shift rather than an automatic car, use your emergency brake when trying to start from a dead stop going up a steep hill – your mastery of the clutch under these extreme conditions may not be up to the job. The speed limit everywhere is 25mph (40kmph) or less, and all passengers must wear seat belts.

3 Underdressing
No matter how sunny it is when you go out in the morning, always take a jacket or a windbreaker. City weather is very variable and it will doubtless be cool, if not cold, damp or wet, by the time you return in the evening.

4 Unsafe Sex
For all its true sexual liberation, unsafe sex is always a no-no in this city that has seen all too clearly what can happen. AIDS and other STDs have been epidemic here. Use a condom.

5 Political Incorrectness
San Francisco is a city where diversity is embraced wholeheartedly, and supporting it is public policy. San Franciscans generally applaud differences of ethnicity, race, age, belief, gender, sexual orientation, and ability. Anyone who mocks or denigrates anyone else for any of these reasons has not understood what makes this city tick.

6 Smoking
California law makes smoking in any enclosed public place illegal – and that includes bars. Smelling cigarette smoke or even seeing someone smoking here is so rare as to be almost non-existent. If you must light up, there are back patios at some clubs where smoking is allowed, and some hotels offer smoking rooms.

7 Panhandlers, Petty Crime and Mugging
San Francisco does have more than its share of homeless people, and many of them do resort to begging. For the most part, they are merely annoying, not dangerous. However, pick-pocketing and purse- and camera-snatching do exist, and it's also true that certain areas should be avoided after dark. However, normal attentiveness should be sufficient.

8 Bad Neighborhoods
Even the seediest neighborhoods are pretty safe in broad daylight, but they, and parks, should be sidestepped at night, when muggings are most likely. That said, there are very few areas that are really perilous within the city, and virtually none in areas that a tourist is likely to frequent.

9 Forgetting to Tip
Restaurant waiting staff depend on their tips to make a living – the salary paid is barely a tenth of what is needed to make ends meet. The usual gratuity is 15 percent, though you can reduce it to 10 percent if the service was not to your liking. Taxi drivers should be tipped about 15 percent, and hotel staff should receive $1 whenever they provide any sort of service.

10 Age Restrictions and ID
If you're over 21 but look younger, carry an ID with you showing your age if you want to try out some of the bars and clubs in town or want to drink alcohol in a restaurant or a shop. You must be over 18 to buy cigarettes.

 Curbing your wheels when parking in the city is law-enforced – you will receive a fine if you fail to follow the practice.

Left **Discount museum tickets** Right **Discount ticket agency**

Streetsmart

TOP 10 Budget Tips

1 Discount Air Tickets

In these days of deregulation and airlines squeezing out travel agencies, finding bargain flights is anybody's game. Most people find that the best bet is the Internet, but don't fail to contact local and national discount shops, too.

2 Hotel Deals

Again, trawl the Internet and sound out your local agencies to see what sort of promotions might be out there. Many hotels offer some fantastic bargains at certain times of the year.

3 Fly-Drive Packages

This sort of offer is somewhat superfluous if your main purpose is to get to know the city and little else outside it. However, if you want to dive into the fruit of that often vine in the Wine Country *(see pp32–5)* or into the waves of the blue Pacific Ocean in Santa Cruz, Monterey, and Carmel *(see pp78–9)*, a car is a necessity. You may be able to negotiate a lower rate if you rent the car for only part of your stay.

4 Discount Coupons

The best discount coupon of them all is the CityPass *(see p134)*, which saves you a bundle, especially on public transportation, if your stay is for about a

week. It currently incorporates nine additional attractions, including admission to the Exploratorium *(see p94)*, SFMOMA *(see pp26–9)*, the California Academy of Sciences *(see pp22–3)*, and more, and the number of sponsoring attractions is increasing. ⬥ www.citypass.com

5 Cheaper Sleeps

Hostels, regardless of your age, are an excellent alternative in San Francisco. There are two locations run by Hosteling International, one in Downtown and the other between Fisherman's Wharf and the Marina *(see p148)*. ⬥ *American Youth Hostels: (415) 863-1444 • www. norcalhostels.org*

6 Cheaper Eateries

San Francisco has an amazing number of low-priced joints that often serve wonderful food. At some of the Mexican places in the Mission, for example, you can still fill up on delicious *burritos*, *tacos*, and the like, for under $5.00. Chinese restaurants are also usually good value.

7 Picnics

With so many clean, beautiful parks, having a picnic lunch is always a delightful option. There are plenty of deli-supermarkets, such as the Real Food Company and the California

Harvest Ranch Market, which carry a fantastic selection of gourmet delectables. ⬥ *Real Food Company: 3939 24th St, 1001 Stanyan St, 2140 Polk St & 3060 Fillmore St • California Harvest Ranch Market: 2285 Market St between Sanchez & Noe*

8 Public Transport Passes

Muni offers 1-day, 3-day, 7-day, and 1-month passes, all at great savings compared to paying $1.10 per ride on the buses and streetcars and $5 per ride on the cable cars *(see p134)*.

9 Communications

Many services provide toll-free numbers when calling within the US from any phone – most of them begin with 800, 877, or 888. Buying phone cards to use for making toll calls can mean great savings. Internet access is free at the New Main Library and at CompUSA. ⬥ *New Main Library: 100 Larkin St; (415) 557-4400; www.sfpl. lib.ca.us • CompUSA: 750 Market St; (415) 391-9778*

10 Laundromats

Since so many San Franciscans are apartment dwellers, nearly every block has a cheap laundromat handy. Wash cycles run about 15-20 minutes and dryers 20–30 minutes. Watch your things, however, since theft is not unknown.

136
For discounted hotel rates in the city, visit the website www.san-francisco-hotels.com

Left **Disabled parking bay** Right **Muni streetcar**

🔟 Special Needs Tips

1 Unlimited Free Parking

Nowhere provides more advanced facilities for the disabled than San Francisco. There are specially marked reserved spots for disabled parking, usually with a blue-and-white wheelchair sign and a blue curb. Often there's a blue-and-white wheelchair stenciled on the pavement, too. There's no charge for parking, either in these spaces or any other, as long as you display a disabled placard. ✆ *Department of Motor Vehicles • 1377 Fell Street • (800) 777-0133*

2 Special Prices

In addition to free parking for the disabled, all Bay Area transit companies offer discounted fares for disabled passengers, including BART, Muni, AC Transit, and Golden Gate Transit. National parks issue special passes for the disabled that entitle them and passengers in the same vehicle to enter free. In addition, many attractions offer reduced entrance fees to the disabled. ✆ *BART Passes Office • (510) 464-7133*

3 Required Accessibility

The San Francisco Convention and Visitors Bureau *(see p132)* publishes a free guide that indicates which hotels comply with the American Disabilities Act.

However, if you want to know the specifics, you should call in advance and ask a few pointed questions. In general, the newer the hotel, the more it is geared up to meet special needs.

4 "Kneeling" Buses

Only some of the Muni city buses have this feature, whereby the bus can be hydraulically lowered, allowing wheelchair-bound people to board, and then be secured in a special part of the bus. The "Muni Access Guide" will give you pointers on how to make the most of the system, and it is free from Muni Accessible Services.

5 Ramped Curbs

Wherever you go, all over town you will find that all the sidewalks have been provided with ramped access, at least at intersections, if not for every driveway as well. Ramped access is also standard for every major public building, including museums, concert halls, big hotels, government buildings, even ferries.

6 Accessible Toilets

Disabled-accessible toilets are provided in many places, including large hotels and restaurants, attractions, and municipal areas. Some are inside the buildings, but there are also a number on the street – the green kiosks that you

can find at Pier 39, at Castro and Market Streets, and at the Civic Center, for example.

7 Independent Living Resource Center

This organization can provide every sort of information you might need about services for travelers with mobility problems, as well as for those with developmental disabilities. ✆ *649 Mission St • (415) 543-6222 • www.ilrcsf.org*

8 Braille Institute of San Francisco

This volunteer organization can provide you with information about accommodations, museums, and other attractions that offer Braille placards and postings. ✆ *1-800-272-4553*

9 Crisis Line for the Handicapped

A 24-hour hotline for persons who have disabilities or their helpers. It provides on-the-spot advice on any subject that might come up during a visit to the city. ✆ *1-800-426-4263*

10 Muni Accessible Services

If you have any questions about public transportation in the city, this is the number to call. This is also the place to obtain your disabled discount card. ✆ *(415) 923-6142 • www.sfmuni.com*

Left **Exchange office sign** Right **ATM machine**

🔟 Banking and Communications

1 Exchange
Exchange offices are found at San Francisco International Airport (see p133), in some Downtown banks, and at American Express and Thomas Cook agencies. However, fees and bad rates of exchange are the norm. It's better to avoid the problem altogether by using ATM machines.

2 ATM Machines
For virtually all travel purposes, this is by far the best way to get cash, either through your home checking account or by securing a PIN number to use with your credit card. The rate of exchange is generally the best for that day, and the small fees charged by the banks are less than those charged by exchange offices. Best of all, you don't have to wait in long lines or carry ID.

3 Credit Cards
Paying with plastic is a way of life in the US. Use cash for small items, but pay for everything else with a credit card, if possible. Most hotels require a credit card number to book a room, and an imprint of one upon checking in. And you will not be able to rent a car without one. If your card is lost or stolen, call the toll-free number of your company and you will not be responsible for any further charges made.

4 Travelers' Checks
Nowadays these are more of a nuisance than a convenience. Cashing them in banks and exchange offices can be a time-consuming hassle. However, if you buy them in dollars, they're the same as cash and can be used for goods and services of any sort – but you may need photo ID.

5 US Currency
US banknotes can be confusing because they're all the same size and color. They come in denominations of $1, $5, $20, $50, and $100, each with a different Founding Father or US president pictured. The coins are easier, being different from each other. The 1-cent coin (or penny) is copper-colored; the 5-cent coin (nickel) is nickel-colored; the 10-cent coin (dime) and the larger 25-cent coin (quarter) are silver-colored.

6 Post Offices
Most US post offices are open from 9am to 5:30pm Monday to Friday and 9am to 2pm on Saturdays. Stamps can be purchased here, from some hotels, and from vending machines. If you need to mail something other than postcards and letters, wait in line at the nearest post office. Otherwise, drop your stamped mail off at the hotel desk or in any street mailbox.

7 Telephones
San Francisco's area code is 415, but neighboring localities have other codes. If you are calling from within the same area, you do not dial the area code; conversely, if you are calling from outside the area, you must dial the area code and precede it with a "1." From pay phones, calls cost 35 cents and up. Toll-free numbers start with 800, 877, 888, or several new similar prefixes. For directory information, dial 411. International calls should be preceded by 011.

8 Voice Mail
The use of this service has reached epidemic proportions in the US, and you may find that you rarely, or never, rouse an actual person on the other end of many calls. Leave a message, with a call-back number, then hope for the best.

9 Internet
There are many cafés that offer internet services around town, usually for about $10 per hour.

10 Courier Services
FedEx and UPS serve international needs, but you should also be aware that the US Post Office offers overnight delivery, both to major cities within the US and to selected cities abroad, and at much more reasonable costs.

There are $2 bills and $1 coins in circulation in the US but they turn up very rarely.

Left **San Francisco ambulance** Right **Police car**

🔟 Security and Health

1 Earthquake Procedures

Should an earthquake strike, stay calm. If you are indoors, a good spot to stand is under a doorframe. If driving, stay in your car and park in an open place, not under a bridge or viaduct. If outside, try to get to an open area. Major quakes are rare, but minor ones happen all the time and are mostly harmless.

2 Consulates

Most major countries have consulates in the city. If anything untoward occurs, contact your national representative.

3 Petty Crime

This sort of thing does exist, so it's best to avert the danger before it arrives by being aware of your surroundings. Don't walk into less than salubrious areas, especially after dark, unless you're sure of where you're going or you're in a group.

4 911

Dial this number whenever an emergency of any sort comes up. It's a free call from any phone. Be sure to have all the information ready – where you are and what has happened – so they know which service to send out to you.

5 AIDS

This virus is still very much a public health problem. Throughout the Bay Area there are ample free public health responses with a range of services, including free check-ups. Your part is not to take risks – use a condom. ✪ AIDS-HIV Nightline: (415) 434-2437 (English only) • California AIDS Foundation Hotline: 1-800-367-2437 or (415) 863-2437 (multilingual)

6 Helplines

A number of helplines exist to provide support and information for almost any problem. ✪ SF Rape Treatment Center: (415) 821-3222 • Suicide Prevention: (415) 781-0500 • Victims of Crime Resource Center: 1-800-842-8467 • New Leaf (for gays, transgender, lesbians, and bisexuals): (415) 626-7000

7 Police Reports

If you are the victim of a crime of any sort, you should report it at your nearest police department. This is especially true if it involves the loss of money or any valuables, including credit cards, as you will need a copy of the police report in order to make a claim against your insurance.

8 Clinics

Walk-in emergency clinics can be found all around town. ✪ Physician Access Center: 26 California St; (415) 397-2881 • Wall Medical Group: 2001 Union St; (415) 447-6800

9 Hospitals

San Francisco has several major hospitals, located in various districts. ✪ Davies Medical Center: Castro St at Duboce; (415) 565-6060 • St Francis Memorial Hospital: 900 Hyde St; (415) 353-6300 • San Francisco General Hospital: 1001 Potrero Ave; (415) 206-8111

10 Health Insurance Claims

Unless you go to one of the free clinics, you will have to pay for any type of health care you receive, and you will usually have to arrange for such payment before you actually receive the treatment. Also confirm that the hospital or clinic you are using accepts your form of coverage.

Consulates

Australia
(415) 536-1970

Canada
(415) 834-3180

France
(415) 397-4330

Germany
(415) 775-1061

Ireland
(415) 392-4214

The Netherlands
(650) 403-0073

New Zealand
(415) 399-1255

United Kingdom
(415) 617-1300

Before you leave home make sure you understand how payments and/or reimbursements on your health insurance are handled.

Left **Picture market, Union Square** Right **Japan Center**

🔟 Shopping Tips

1 Department Stores

The big guns are all well represented in this city that loves looking good. Most of them are clustered around Union Square. The more upscale the department store, the more it feels like the exclusive parlor of some deluxe hotel, where you are the pampered guest. A very comfortable way to shop *(see pp50–51)*.

2 Boutiques

The smaller shops generally feature more interesting and quirky merchandise – not counting all the international boutiques that also circle Union Square. Some of the more offbeat neighborhoods, such as Hayes Valley *(see p100)*, offer some really original designs, often by local or regional talents.

3 Malls

There are no real American-style malls in San Francisco. The ones that come closest are the San Francisco Shopping Center *(see p51)* and the Crocker Galleria *(see p50)*. Other centers are in historic structures such as Ghirardelli and The Cannery *(see pp12–13)*, or have architectural originality, such as the Embarcadero Center *(see p50)* and the Japan Center *(see p99)*. You will find unusual shops in most of them.

4 Flea Markets and Thrift Shops

This sort of shopping can net you some real treasures and keep your bank account intact, too. One of the most central flea markets is in Bernal Heights. Thrift shops are all over town – two of the best are located in the Mission, the Good-will Store and the Salvation Army Thrift Store. Both offer everything from vintage clothing to miscellaneous junk.
🅢 *Alemany Flea Market: 100 Alemany Blvd at US 101, Bernal Heights • Goodwill Store: 1580 Mission St • Salvation Army Thrift Store: 1500 Valencia St*

5 Garage and Sidewalk Sales

A thoroughly enjoyable custom that can unearth some surprising plunder in a city with so much style. To find a good garage sale, keep an eye out for announcements tacked to telephone poles, or take a weekend stroll in one of the likelier neighborhoods – such as the Haight, the Castro, and the Mission.

6 Bargaining

In established outlets bargaining is out of the question. However, in flea markets, garage sales, and some of the funkier ethnic stores, it is acceptable. Make a counter offer and haggle it down to a mutually satisfactory sum.

7 Sales Tax

In the US sales tax is added to your total bill, rather than included in the listed price, apart from groceries. In San Francisco, the sales tax is currently 8.5 percent, and hotel tax is 14 percent. However, tax varies from state to state.

8 Corner Stores

Every two blocks or so all around the city, except in the most exclusive neighborhoods, there are corner stores that sell a little bit of everything – some fresh produce, maybe some deli items, a few pharmaceuticals, toiletry necessities, and general groceries. Just be aware that you pay as much as 50 percent more for everything you buy here.

9 Refunds

If you have second thoughts about something you bought, you have a right to return it for a refund. If it is defective, you are entitled to a replacement or a refund.

10 California Attorney General's Office Public Inquiry Unit

If you have been dealt with by a retailer or service-provider in an illegal way, you can take your complaint here so that court proceedings can be initiated or other sanctions put into effect.
🅢 *1-800-952-5225*

For any unresolved complaints on a product you have purchased, call the Better Business Bureau on (866) 411-2221.

Left **Hotel grading sign** Center **Ice cream cake** Right **Clam chowder and sourdough bread**

🔟 Eating and Accommodation Tips

1 California Cuisine

With over 5,000 places to dine and/or drink in the city, you know that food is important to San Franciscans. It's a moot point whether so-called "fusion" cuisine got its start in the city some decades ago but it has certainly reached its apotheosis here – with all the international influences, it was inevitable that chefs would begin borrowing and melding ingredients, flavors, and methods from a broad mélange of international styles. The result is California Cuisine.

2 Other Cuisines

It would be difficult to think of an authentic national cuisine that is not represented by at least one restaurant in the city. That includes Tibetan, Eritrean, Afghan, Kurdish, and Bolivian, as well as the more standard Thai, Vietnamese, Russian, and most European countries.

3 Reservations

If you're hankering after a fancy meal in one of the more famous restaurants, you'd do best to call in advance, sometimes up to two months ahead in the case of one or two of the top Bay Area draws. For the middling places, making a reservation a day or two before should suffice, unless you choose a weekend night.

4 Drinks

Good restaurants have *sommeliers*, so you can usually depend on their wine choices to go with what you have ordered. If you choose your own wine, remember that California wines are identified by grape rather than by region. If beer is more your thing, there are excellent local brews that compete very well with the best European products. And don't forget to try the local mineral waters *(see p67)*.

5 Tax and Tipping

Sales tax applies to restaurants, so 8.5 percent will be added to your total check. You should leave at least a 15 percent tip *(see p135)*. You may add the tip to your credit card slip, or leave it in cash on the table.

6 Choosing Hotel Locations

Do you want to be right in the heart of the action? Do you want a view of the Bay? Do you want to experience one of the unique neighborhoods? Once you've decided, you can zero in on the right price-range *(see pp142–9)*.

7 Hotel Gradings

Accommodations of every sort are to be found in the city and its environs. There is a star-based grading system, which pertains to certain amenities, such as telephone, TV, frigobar, etc.

8 Making Hotel Reservations

San Francisco generally fills up quickly in almost every price category, so don't waste a moment securing a reservation. Telephone bookings are accepted with a valid credit card, although some may require a fax before confirming.

9 Extra Costs and Tipping

Parking at Downtown hotels is almost always extra, paid on a per night basis, and a flat fee of up to $1 is charged for each phone call made from the room, even if it is a toll-free number. Anything you consume from a frigobar will be surcharged. You will receive an itemized bill when you check out. Tipping is important for any service provided *(see p135)*.

10 Traveling with Kids

Many hotels levy no extra charge for children under 12 staying in their parents' room, and some raise the age as high as 18 – ask in advance. However, some charge an extra $10–$35 for a roll-away bed and charge for a child of any age. Some of the best family-friendly accommodations are found among the motels along the Marina and in the Fisherman's Wharf area, where parking is usually included too.

Left **Fairmont Hotel** Right **Mark Hopkins Inter-Continental**

🔟 Hilltop Hotels

1 The Ritz-Carlton
If you want the ultimate in luxury and thoughtful service, this is the place to come. The views from the perfectly appointed rooms are magnificent, the staff at the top of their game, and the food sublime. ✆ 600 Stockton St • Map N4 • (415) 296-7465
• www.ritzcarlton.com
• Dis. access • $$$$$

2 Mark Hopkins Inter-Continental
The Top of the Mark restaurant is a major pull, of course, with its 360-degree panorama, and the service is genuinely caring. The rooms are provided with every amenity and achieve an excellent standard of comfort. ✆ 1 Nob Hill
• Map N3 • (415) 392-3434
• www.markhopkins.net
• Dis. access • $$$$

3 Fairmont
"Opulent" and "palatial" barely begin to describe this *grande dame* of San Francisco hotels, taking pride of place on Nob Hill. The rooms and service are commensurate with its status. ✆ 950 Mason St
• Map N3 • (415) 772-5000
• www.fairmont.com
• Dis. access • $$$$

4 Renaissance Stanford Court
Long a business favorite, it's just near the top of Nob Hill and handy to everything Downtown. The stained-glass dome in the lobby gives it a grand feel. Marble baths and canopy beds in some rooms, complimentary limousine service, and every comfort seen to. ✆ 905 California St • Map N3 • (415) 989-3500
• www.renaissancehotels. com • $$$$

5 Huntington
Situated at the top of Nob Hill, across from Grace Cathedral, this hotel is like staying in the clubby apartment of a rich uncle with impeccable taste. The rooms are luxurious, there's an excellent restaurant, and a spa where you can get a champagne facial. ✆ 1075 California St • Map N3 • (415) 474-5400
• www.huntingtonhotel. com • $$$$

6 Laurel Inn
This stylish hotel is located in Presidio Heights, and is decorated in a hip mid-century fashion. The 18 bedrooms have kitchenettes and some feature CD players and VCRs. Breakfast is included and there is free parking. ✆ 444 Presidio Ave • Map E3 • (415) 567-8467 • www.jdvhospitality. com • Dis. access • $$$

7 Hotel Drisco
This Pacific Heights property is one of the Leading Small Hotels of the World, and, although the elegance is perhaps a little too understated, it delivers on service. Details include complimentary breakfast and morning newspaper – and some of the very best vistas in the city. ✆ 2901 Pacific Ave • Map E2 • (415) 346-2880
• www.hoteldrisco.com
• Dis. access • $$$

8 Queen Anne
Built in 1890, this old mansion has been lovingly refurbished according to Victorian taste. Rooms are all different and filled with antiques. Breakfast is complimentary, and your morning newspaper, too. The views are delightful. ✆ 1590 Sutter at Octavia
• Map F3 • (415) 441-2828
• www.queenanne.com
• Dis. access • $$

9 Alta Mira
This old-fashioned hotel offers sweeping views of both the Bay and the city. Many of the rooms have balconies. ✆ 125 Bulkley Ave, Sausalito
• (415) 332-1350 • $

10 Claremont Resort and Spa
This country club-style resort was built in 1915 and has the feel of that era, newly restored. There are business services, a fitness center, two pools, tennis courts, and views of Golden Gate Bridge. ✆ 41 Tunnel Rd, Berkeley • (510) 843-3000 • www.claremont resort.com • Dis. access
• $$$

Note: Unless otherwise stated, all hotels accept credit cards, and have en-suite bathrooms and air conditioning

Price Categories

For a standard, double room per night (with breakfast if included), taxes and extra charges.	$ under $100
	$$ $100–$200
	$$$ $200–$250
	$$$$ $250–$300
	$$$$$ over $300

Above **Lobby, Hyatt Regency**

Traditional Hotels

1 Mandarin Oriental
Located on the top 11 floors of Downtown's third-tallest building, this is one of the classiest hotels in the city. Its East-meets-West decor is magnificent, its restaurant one of the finest, and the rooms, amenities, and service superb. ◈ 222 Sansome St • Map N5 • (415) 276-9888 • www.mandarinoriental. com • Dis. access • $$$$$

2 The Pan Pacific
Marble bathrooms, some with Jacuzzis, and the fluffiest bathrobes are just some of the comforts at this daringly designed modern hotel. The atrium lobby towers 17 stories high, with a glass elevator. Free use of towncars is a special plus. ◈ 500 Post St • Map P3 • (415) 771-8600 • www.panpacific.com • Dis. access • $$$$

3 Palace
Dating from 1875, this historic landmark emanates an aura of architectural splendor that nevertheless whispers refinement. The stupefyingly gorgeous Garden Court and the original Maxfield Parrish mural in the Pied Piper Lounge are national treasures. The rooms are wonderful, too, but sadly without views. ◈ 2 New Montgomery St • Map P5 • (415) 512-1111 • www. sfpalace.com • Dis. access • $$$

4 Park Hyatt
This is the smallest and most luxurious of the four city Hyatts, and it is situated very near the waterfront. Rooms have good views of the Bay Bridge or the city, if you get the right ones. You'll find that staff greet you by name and the rooms have personal touches. ◈ 333 Battery St • Map N5 • (415) 392-1234 • www. parksanfrancisco.hyatt.com • Dis. access • $$$$

5 Sir Francis Drake
Where the doormen wear Beefeater costumes and the cable cars glide by constantly. This splendid Art Deco landmark is just a block off Union Square. All in all, a very festive and colorful feel, both in the public and private rooms. ◈ 450 Powell St • Map P4 • (415) 392-7755 • www.sirfrancis drake.com • Dis. access • $$$

6 Hotel Nikko
High-tech and minimalist white marble interiors radiate modernity in this Japanese-style environment. Its cool comfort and tranquil luxury, such as silk wallpaper, soothe the spirit and free the mind. The excellent Anzu restaurant creates the same peaceful atmosphere. ◈ 222 Mason St • Map Q3 • (415) 394-1111 • www. hotelnikkosf.com • Dis. access • $$$

7 Hyatt Regency
The 15-story lobby has long plants trailing down, a waterfall, and glass elevators. Try the revolving restaurant on the roof for its views. ◈ 50 Drumm St • Map N6 • (415) 788-1234 • www. sanfranciscoregencyhyatt. com • Dis. access • $$$

8 Four Seasons
Designed with the expense-account traveler in mind, this place has thought of every sort of business amenity, including two phone lines and a high-speed Internet connection in each room. ◈ 757 Market St • Map P4 • (415) 633-3000 • www. fourseasons.com • Dis. access • $$$$$

9 The Westin St Francis
This grand San Francisco institution still shines in its lovely public rooms, but it's become a tour-group mediocrity otherwise. The tower rooms do have phenomenal views, however. ◈ 335 Powell St • Map P4 • (415) 397-7000 • www.westin. com • Dis. access • $$$

10 Ritz-Carlton Resort
A rambling mansion on its own verdant bluff, overlooking the Pacific. The perfect retreat from which to enjoy the Bay Area. ◈ 1 Miramontes Point Rd, Half Moon Bay • (650) 712-7000 • www. ritzcarlton.com • Dis. access • $$$$$

Left **Campton Place** Right **The Clift**

TOP10 Boutique Hotels

1 Campton Place
A member of the Leading Small Hotels of the World and definitely one of San Francisco's finest, this place aims to provide personal attention to every guest. Expect to find the best of everything. Its restaurant also has national ranking. *340 Stockton St • Map P4 • (415) 781-5555 • www.camptonplace.com • Dis. access • $$$$$*

2 Monaco
In the heart of the Theater District, this quirky but extremely comfortable hotel is run to perfection. The fairy-tale decor is joyously original, being at once a celebration of color and elegance, and the beds may be the most comfortable in the world. The stylish restaurant is an attraction in itself. *501 Geary St • Map P3 • (415) 292-0100 • www.monaco-sf.com • Dis. access • $$$*

3 W
Talk about trendy in this town and all conversations will lead to the W hotel. Minimalist with luxury touches throughout. Rooms have cordless phones and CD players. The clientele that come for drinks and general confabulation are modish trendsetters too. *181 3rd St • Map Q5 • (415) 777-5300 • www.starwoodhotels.com • Dis. access • $$$$*

4 The Clift
"Equal parts wit, surrealism, and glamour." So say the proprietors of this latest Ian Schrager property, with interiors by Philippe Starck. You'll laugh with delight at the visual jokes, including a chaise very, very longue by none other than Dalí. *495 Geary St • Map P3 • (415) 775-4700 • www.morganshotelgroup.com • Dis. access • $$$*

5 Triton
Perhaps the city's most original hotel, featuring avant-garde touches – evening tarot card readings, feather boa rentals, and several suites designed by rock celebrities, including Jerry Garcia. It's all too cool for words; you might run into Cher or Courtney Love, both of whom have stayed here. *342 Grant Ave • Map P4 • (415) 394-0500 • www.hoteltriton.com • Dis. access • $$*

6 Rex
Steeped in California's literary and artistic traditions, this great little hotel boasts an intellectual air and decor that suggest 1920s salon society. Still, the rooms have the very latest touches, such as voice mail, CD players, and writing desks for guests to pursue their own creativity. *562 Sutter St • Map P3 • (415) 433-4434 • www.thehotelrex.com • Dis. access • $$$*

7 The Maxwell
This beautiful Art Deco hotel dates from 1908 and has a handsome style, accented by Edward Hopper prints. Parking is offered – a great rarity. *386 Geary St • Map P3 • (415) 986-2000 • www.maxwellhotel.com • Dis. access • $$*

8 The Inn Above Tide
The only hotel built directly on the Bay. The views from guestroom balconies are stunning, and the ambience serene. A wonderful choice, convenient to the city via the Golden Gate Bridge or a ferry ride. *30 El Portal, Sausalito • (415) 332-9535 • www.innabovetide.com • Dis. access • $$$*

9 Mill Valley Inn
Combining the sophistication of a European hotel with the cozy charm of a California mill town, this inn is tucked away in a redwood grove. *165 Throckmorton Ave, Mill Valley • (415) 389-6608 • www.marinhotels.com • $$*

10 Garden Court Hotel
Newly remodeled guestrooms feature private terraces in this Spanish-style hotel. *520 Cowper St, Palo Alto • (650) 322-9000 • www.gardencourt.com • Dis. access • $$$*

Note: *Unless otherwise stated, all hotels accept credit cards, and have en-suite bathrooms and air conditioning*

Price Categories

For a standard,	
double room per	$ under $100
night (with breakfast	$$ $100–$200
if included), taxes	$$$ $200–$250
and extra charges.	$$$$ $250–$300
	$$$$$ over $300

Above **The Red Victorian**

B&Bs and Guesthouses

1 White Swan Inn

This quaint B&B is like a country inn in the heart of Downtown with bright floral prints and Victorian-style canopied beds. Champagne in the late afternoon and a great English breakfast are complimentary. ❧ *845 Bush St • Map N3 • (415) 775-1755 • www. whiteswaninnsf.com • No air conditioning • $$*

2 The Union Street Inn

Combining the elegance and gentility of an Edwardian home, just up from the Marina and right on fashionable Union Street. The individually decorated rooms are all spacious, with original antiques and art, fine linens, and complimentary chocolates, fresh flowers, and fruit. ❧ *2229 Union St • Map E2 • (415) 346-0424 • www.unionstreetinn.com • No air conditioning • $$*

3 Archbishop's Mansion

Built for San Francisco's archbishop in 1904, this converted wonder is a slice of city history, and has the Alamo Square views that appear on postcards. Free breakfast and evening wine and cheese make it a real treat. Be aware, however, that the neighborhood is rundown. ❧ *1000 Fulton St • Map F3 • (415) 563-7872 • www.jdvhospitality.com • $$*

4 The Red Victorian

Inspired along hippie ideals, you meet the owners and other guests and engage in intelligent conversation around the breakfast table. Each guestroom is also designed to celebrate an aspect of world love. ❧ *1665 Haight St • Map E4 • (415) 864-1978 • www. redvic.com • No air conditioning • $*

5 Inn 1890

Located in Haight Ashbury, this Queen Anne-style building dates back to 1890. This cozy hotel has hardwood floors, bay windows, and fireplaces. The spacious guest rooms have brass or iron queen-sized beds with oversized comforters, bathrobes, and slippers. ❧ *1890 Page St • Map D4 • (415) 386-0486 • www.inn1890.com • No air conditioning • $$$*

6 Alamo Square Inn

Handsome Queen Anne and Tudor Revival homes constitute this charming B&B, restored with impeccable taste. Both overlook the famous square with its even more famous view. A complimentary American breakfast is served in the sunny (fog permitting) conservatory. Smoking is allowed on the back patio only. Free off-street parking. ❧ *719 Scott St • Map E4 • (415) 922-2055 • www. alamosquareinn.com • No air conditioning • $*

7 Albion House Inn

The nine rooms here are all cozily decorated and have names such as The Cabrillo Room and the Sir Francis Suite. Janis Joplin *(see p55)* used to stay in the Joplin Room, which has its own sundeck. ❧ *135 Gough St • Map F4 • (415) 621-0896 • www.albionhouseinn.com • $$*

8 Panama Hotel

A friendly, eccentric place, filled with period eclectic touches. Rooms have names such as the Bordello Room, and Friend's of Dorothy – each with its own tale to tell. ❧ *4 Bayview St, San Rafael • (415) 457-3993 • www.panamahotel.com • No air conditioning • $$*

9 The Pelican Inn

Majestically positioned deep in a valley, each of the seven rooms has antiques, and a roaring fire is lit every day in the inglenook fireplace. ❧ *Muir Beach • (415) 383-6000 • www. pelicaninn.com • No air conditioning • $$$*

10 Cliff Crest B&B Inn

Surrounded by redwoods, the rooms in this Queen Anne Victorian are graced with fresh flowers, and some have views of the Bay. ❧ *407 Cliff St, Santa Cruz • (831) 252-1057 • www.cliffcrestinn.com • No air conditioning • Dis. access • $$*

Left **Hotel del Sol** Right **Edward II Inn and Pub**

TOP 10 Neighborhood Hotels

1 Hotel Del Sol

Called "festive and spacious," this place really is a ray of sunshine. Bright colors and cheerful patterns greet you around every corner, and the staff is just a nice as can be. An especially great place to bring the kids. ✆ *3100 Webster St • Map E2 • (415) 921-5520 • www. thehoteldelsol.com • No air conditioning • $$*

2 Edward II Inn and Pub

Located just up from the Marina, this is a real find if you want to be close to the sights, although the street tends to be very busy. Nevertheless, this truly charming 1914 Edwardian inn features rooms full of antiques and fresh flowers, and serves complimentary afternoon drinks and *hors d'oeuvres*, as well as breakfast. ✆ *3155 Scott St at Lombard • Map E2 • (415) 922-3000 • www. edwardii.com • Dis. access • $$*

3 Marina Motel

Tucked away in a flower-filled Mediterranean courtyard decorated with murals, this motel offers guests a peaceful oasis right in the heart of the beautiful Marina District. Rooms are simple and clean, and parking is included. ✆ *2576 Lombard St • Map E2 • (415) 921-9406 or 1-800 346-6118 • www.marinamotel.com • $*

4 Stanyan Park Hotel

Listed on the National Register of Historic Places, this noble Victorian has been receiving guests since 1904. Right on Golden Gate Park. Decorated in period style, breakfast and afternoon tea are included. ✆ *750 Stanyan St • Map D4 • (415) 751-1000 • www.stanyanpark. com • No air conditioning • Dis. access • $$*

5 Phoenix Hotel

The place that Johnny Depp, REM, and the late John F. Kennedy, Jr, have all chosen to stay when they've visited the city might be to your liking, too. Located a bit too close to the Tenderloin for all but the most self-assured. Breakfast included, as well as parking. ✆ *601 Eddy St • Map Q2 • (415) 776-1380 • www.jdvhospitality.com • Dis. access • $$*

6 Tuscan Inn

It's a Best Western, but one of the stylish ones. Located right in Fisherman's Wharf, staying here takes some of the touristy edge off the neighborhood. Features include a mirrored wall in each room, free coffee, tea, and biscuits, and a complimentary limousine service. ✆ *425 North Point St • Map K3 • (415) 561-1100 • www.tuscaninn.com • Dis. access • $$*

7 Seal Rock Inn

Handy for Cliff House and Land's End *(see p115)*, as well as the Palace of the Legion of Honor. Rooms are large, though plain, and there's free parking and a heated pool. ✆ *545 Point Lobos Ave • Map A3 • (415) 752-8000 • www.sealrockinn.com • $$*

8 Jackson Court

Located in Pacific Heights, this is a magnificent 1900 brownstone mansion. The wood-paneled parlor is an inviting place, and the stone fireplace provides a warm glow for afternoon tea. ✆ *2198 Jackson St • Map F2 • (415) 929-7670 • www.jacksoncourt. com • $$$*

9 Twin Peaks Hotel

Clean, quiet and comfortable, but it doesn't get any simpler than this. The advantage is the close proximity to the Castro, Hayes Valley, and the Mission. ✆ *2160 Market St • Map F4 • (415) 863-2909 • No en-suite bathrooms • No air conditioning • $*

10 Pacific Heights Inn

Situated on a quiet block close to transportation, this 1960s motel is modern and comfortable. There is on-site parking and some rooms have kitchenettes. ✆ *1555 Union St • Map F2 • (415) 776-3310 • www. pacificheightsinn.com • No air conditioning • $*

***Note:** Unless otherwise stated, all hotels accept credit cards, and have en-suite bathrooms and air conditioning*

Price Categories

For a standard, double room per night (with breakfast if included), taxes and extra charges.

$	under $100
$$	$100–$200
$$$	$200–$250
$$$$	$250–$300
$$$$$	over $300

Above **Inn on Castro**

🔟 Gay and Lesbian Hotels

1 Inn on Castro

The very friendly owner/operator of this B&B seems to have thought of everything to make your stay in the heart of the Castro as pleasurable as possible. He's ready with maps and advice on where to go. Comfort is key, in bright rooms filled with art and plants. ❖ 321 Castro St • Map E5 • (415) 861-0321 • www.innon castro2.com • No air conditioning • Dis. access • $$

2 Chateau Tivoli

Rooms and suites in this stunning old building are named after Mark Twain, Enrico Caruso, Jack London, and others, to remind guests of San Francisco's illustrious history in the arts. Rooms are furnished with four-poster beds, fireplaces, bay windows, American Renaissance pieces, and the like. ❖ 1057 Steiner St • Map E3 • (415) 776-5462 • www.chateautivoli.com • No air conditioning • $$

3 The Willows Inn

This restored 1903 Edwardian house is conveniently located close to public transport in Castro's gay community. The interior is a blend of handcrafted willow furnishings, antique dressers, armoires, and cozy comforters. ❖ 710 14th St • Map E4 • (415) 431-4770 • www.willowssf.com • No en-suite bathrooms • No air conditioning • $$

4 24 Henry Guesthouse

This charming building was constructed in the Victorian style in the late 1880s. It is situated on a quiet, tree-lined street just three blocks from the Castro. All of the six rooms have high ceilings and period furniture. Guests can enjoy free wireless internet connection and a complimentary breakfast. ❖ 24 Henry St • Map F4 • (415) 864-5686, (800) 900-5684 • www.24henry.com • No air conditioning • $

5 Castro Suites

This restored 1890s Italianate Victorian has views of Downtown and the Bay. Accommodations are a mixture of contemporary furniture, original art, and plants. The kitchen is equipped with dishwasher, clothes washer, and microwave. ❖ 927 14th St • Map E4 • (415) 437-1783 • www. castrosuites.com • No air conditioning • Dis. access • $$

6 Renoir Hotel

A friendly, gay boutique hotel with the best views of the annual gay pride march on Market Street. Built in 1909, it was restored to its turn-of-the-20th-century charm in 2001. It has a bar, lounge, and café. ❖ 45 McAllister St • Map Q3 • (415) 626-5200 • www.hotelrenoirsanfran cisco.com • No air conditioning • $$

7 The Inn San Francisco

This fine Victorian mansion serves a buffet breakfast in charming double parlors. The garden has a redwood hot tub, and sundeck with a panoramic view of the city. ❖ 943 South Van Ness St • Map F5 • (415) 641-0188 • www. innsf.com • No air conditioning • $

8 The Parker House

This Edwardian mini-mansion has expansive gardens and sun decks. Just steps away from gay bars and restaurants. ❖ 520 Church St • Map F5 • (415) 621-3222 • www. parkerguesthouse.com • No air conditioning • $

9 Bel Abri

Rooms feature shutters, French tapestries, and wrought-iron pieces. Most rooms include a fireplace, and two of the rooms also have Jacuzzis. ❖ 837 California Blvd, Napa • (707) 253-2100 • www.belabri. net • Dis. access • $$

10 Meadowlark Inn

In the heart of the Wine Country, this elegant guesthouse is situated on an estate with gardens, meadows, and great facilities such as a mineral pool, hot tub, and whirlpool spa. ❖ 601 Petrified Forest Rd, Calistoga • (707) 942-5651 • www.meadowlarkinn.com • No air conditioning • $$

 San Francisco is, of course, a tolerant city and virtually all hotels will welcome gay and lesbian guests with a smile.

Left **Chelsea Motor Inn** Right **San Remo**

🔟 Budget Hotels and Hostels

1 Coventry Motor Inn
A good, basic motel, offering large pleasant rooms with bay windows, located on the Marina's "Motel Row." It isn't beautiful, but it's functional and reliable. All rooms are no-smoking, and parking is complimentary. A minimum stay may apply on some weekends. ⌖ *1901 Lombard St • Map F2 • (415) 567-1200 • www.coventrymotorinn. com • Dis. access • $*

2 Beck's Motor Lodge
This standard 1960s motel is handy for the Castro, the Lower Haight, and the Mission. It's one of those no-frills, what-you-see-is-what-you-get places, simple and very serviceable, and quiet, given its prime location. Free parking is a plus, and cable TV, too. ⌖ *2222 Market St • Map F4 • (415) 621-8212 • No air conditioning • $*

3 Chelsea Motor Inn
Vaguely English Tudor in style, with a slate roof, the rooms are comfortable and fairly large, and a few have bay windows. The location is convenient to the Marina and Pacific Heights. Free parking, cable TV, and in-room coffee maker. All no-smoking. ⌖ *2095 Lombard St • Map E2 • (415) 563-5600 • www.chelseamotor inn.com • Dis. access • $*

4 Cow Hollow Motor Inn and Suites
Larger-than-average rooms. Floral wallpaper and traditional furniture give it a homey feel. Some suites have Oriental carpets accenting wood floors, marble fireplaces, and antiques. Free parking and a no-smoking floor. ⌖ *2190 Lombard St • Map E2 • (415) 921-5800 • www. cowhollowmotorinn.com • Dis. access • $*

5 Marina Inn
The charm of a San Francisco Victorian awaits you here. The marble lobby is the focal point of this four-story hotel built in 1924, and the sitting room is the setting for Continental breakfasts. After a day's sightseeing, return to the inn for afternoon sherry. ⌖ *3110 Octavia St at Lombard • Map F2 • (415) 928-1000 • www.marinainn.com • No air conditioning • Dis. access • $*

6 San Remo
North Beach's biggest bargain is full of charms. Each room is decorated with antiques, and the corridors feature brass railings and hanging plants under skylights. Every room has its own sink, while other facilities are down the hall. ⌖ *2237 Mason St • Map K3 • (415) 776-8688 • www.sanremohotel.com • No en-suite bathrooms • No air conditioning • $*

7 Union Square Hostel
Action-central for all the major sights. Rooms hold up to five beds. All major public transportation is just outside. Nightly movies, e-mail access, walking tours, an events board, and lots of tourist info are other pluses. ⌖ *312 Mason St • Map P3 • (415) 788-5604 • www. norcalhostels.org • No en-suite bathrooms • No air conditioning • $*

8 Fisherman's Wharf Hostel
On a wooded hilltop, this hostel is housed in Civil War-era buildings. It's just a short walk to everything along the Bayshore. ⌖ *Fort Mason, Bldg. 240 • Map F1 • (415) 771-7277 • www.norcalhostels.org • Dis. access • $*

9 Zen City Center
The center has six comfortable, quiet rooms available for those who are interested in learning about Zen practices. ⌖ *300 Page St • Map F4 • (415) 863-3136 • www. sfzc.org • Dis. access • No en-suite bathrooms • No air conditioning • $*

10 Marin Headlands Hostel
Nearby are the Muir Woods, and great beaches. ⌖ *Fort Barry, Bldg 941, Field & Bunker Rds • (415) 331-2777 • www.hiusa.org • No en-suite bathrooms • No air conditioning • $*

Note: *Unless otherwise stated, all hotels accept credit cards, and have en-suite bathrooms and air conditioning*

Above **Executive Suites**

Price Categories

For a standard, double room per night (with breakfast if included), taxes and extra charges.	**$** under $100
	$$ $100–$200
	$$$ $200–$250
	$$$$ $250–$300
	$$$$$ over $300

🔟 Apartments and Private Homes

1 Oakwood Geary Courtyard

Located close to Union Square and public transport, this modern apartment block includes amenities such as a swimming pool, sauna, concierge, dry cleaning service, fitness center, and business center. The furnished and serviced apartments can be rented for a minimum of 30 days. 🖲 *639 Geary St • Map P4 • (415) 749-0101 • www.oakwood.com • $$*

2 Executive Suites

Furnished apartments are available in several locations around town, with a 30-day minimum stay. This company provides all the comforts of home, with the added amenities of a hotel. Every apartment has a fully equipped kitchen. All utilities are included, as well as local phone calls, cable TV, and maid service. 🖲 *1388 Sutter St • Map P1 • (415) 776-5151 • www.executivesuites-sf.com • Dis. access • $*

3 Grosvenor Suites

An all-suite hotel on Nob Hill. The renovated rooms offer kitchens including refrigerators and microwave. There are housekeeping services, voice mail, cable TV, valet service (nominal fee), and laundry service. 🖲 *899 Pine St • Map N3 • (415) 421-1899 • www.grosvenorsuites.com • Dis. access • $$*

4 Edward II Inn and Suites

Edward II Apartment Suites are across the street from the Edward II Inn *(see p146)*, near the yacht harbor. Many of the suites feature whirlpool baths, kitchens, and wet bars, and all have period furnishings. 🖲 *3155 Scott St at Lombard • Map E2 • (415) 922-3000 • www.edwardii.com • No air conditioning • Dis. access • $$*

5 The Harcourt

Convenient to Downtown. Each room has a private telephone connected to a 24-hour switchboard. Maid service and towel exchange provided weekly. There are also a laundromat and TV viewing rooms, plus a games area. All guests have use of the ice machine, refrigerator, and tea and hot chocolate. 🖲 *1105 Larkin St • Map P2 • (415) 673-7721 • www.harcourthotel.net • No air conditioning • Dis. access • $*

6 Nob Hill Place

A short walk to Downtown, the furnished studios and executive apartments boast superb views and are available for a minimum of 30 days. All rooms include fully equipped kitchens, internet access and cable TV. 🖲 *1155 Jones St • Map N3 • (415) 928-2051 • www.nobhillplace.com • No air conditioning • $$*

7 The Monroe Hotel

A San Francisco Victorian built in 1906. Amid the mansions of Pacific Heights, the Monroe combines the best features of a hotel and an apartment. Included in the price are American-style breakfasts and four-course dinners. Maid service is also provided. 🖲 *1870 Sacramento St • Map N1 • (415) 474-6200 • www.monroeresidenceclub.com • No air conditioning • Dis. access • $*

8 Bed & Breakfast San Francisco

All homes participating in the service have been carefully selected. Private residences in every desirable part of San Francisco are listed, including Pacific Heights and the Marina. 🖲 *1-800-452-8249 or (415) 899-0060 • www.bbsf.com • $–$$, depending on placement*

9 Home Exchange Inc.

Home exchangers simply trade their homes at a time that is convenient to both parties. 🖲 *1-800-877-8723 or (310)798-3864 • www.homeexchange.com*

10 The Invented City

This home exchange agency provides web access to members worldwide who exchange their homes for short and long-term stays. 🖲 *41 Sutter St • (415) 846-7588 • www.invented-city.com*

General Index

Index

Index

Acknowledgments

Main Contributor
Jeffrey Kennedy is a native
San Franciscan, but now lives
mainly in Italy and Spain. A
graduate of Stanford University,
he divides his time between
producing, writing and acting. He
is also co-author of *Top 10 Rome*
and author of *Top 10 Mallorca* and
Top 10 Miami & The Keys.

Produced by Sargasso Media
Ltd, London

Editorial Director Zoë Ross
Art Editor Janis Utton
Picture Research Helen Stallion
Proofreader Stewart J Wild
Indexer Hilary Bird
Editorial Assistance Tracy Becker
Main Photographer Robert Vente
Additional Photography
Neil Lukas, Andrew McKinney,
Trevor Hill
Illustrator chrisorr.com

FOR DORLING KINDERSLEY
Publishing Manager
Ian Midson
Publisher
Douglas Amrine
Revisions Coordinator
Mani Ramaswamy
Assistant Revisions Coordinator
Mary Ormandy
Senior Cartographic Editor
Casper Morris
DTP
Jason Little
Production
Melanie Dowland
Picture Librarians
David Saldanha

**Additional Design and
Editorial Assistance**
Sherry Collins, Nicola Erdpresser,
Sam Merrell, Karen Villabona,
Ros Walford

Maps DK India: Managing Editor
Aruna Ghose; Senior Cartographer
Uma Bhattacharya; Cartographic
Researcher Suresh Kumar.

Special Assistance
The author would like to thank
the following people for their
assistance: Patricia Perez-Arce
and Ed, Sonal Bhatt, Bruce and
Celeste Joki, Margaret Casey and
Mark Trahan, Robert Vente, Angela
Jackson, Sandy Barnes, Harriet
and Rick Lehrbaum, Paul Brown,
Phyllis Butler, Nini Dibble, Jolie
Chain, Helen Craddick, Vivian
Deuschl, Marr Goodrum, and
Isabelle Lejano.

Picture Credits
t-top; tl-top left; tlc-top left center;
tc-top center; tr-top right; cla-
center left above; ca-center above;
cra-center right above; cl-center
left; c-center; cr-center right;
clb-center left below; cb-center
below; crb-center right below; bl-
bottom left; b-bottom; bc-bottom
center; bcl-bottom center left; br-
bottom right; d-detail.

Every effort has been made
to trace the copyright holders
of images, and we apologize in
advance for any unintentional
omissions. We would be
pleased to insert the
appropriate acknowledgments
in any subsequent edition of
this publication.

The publishers would like to
thank the following individuals,
companies and picture libraries
for their kind permission to
reproduce their photographs:

Absinthe Brasserie & Bar: 105tl; Cable Car Museum: 11b; Ed Archie NoiseCat, *Baby Frog, 2001*, Blown and sand-carved glass, 11 x 10 3/4 x 8 inches/Museum of Craft & Folk Art/Lee Fatherree: 42b. BambuddhaLounge.com: 70tl; Bancroft Library/Berkeley University: 36tr, Jan Butchofsky-Houser/ Houserstock: 18t.

California Academy of Science: 22tl, 22tr, 22b, 23b; *California Artist, 1982* © Robert Arneson/VAGA, New York and DACS, London, 2002: 27t; Campton Place Hotel: 114tl; The Clift Hotel/Ian Schrager Hotels/Nikolas Koerno: 114tr;

Corbis: 1, 4–5, 8cl, 9, 10b, 12–13, 14–15, 16tl, 16b, 17c, 17b, 27c, 34t, 36tl, 37tr, 37br, 39, 40tr, 52tl, 52tr, 54tl, 54tr, 54b, 55r, 74b, 76tr, 78tl, 78tr, 79t, 80–81, 86–7, 102–03, 118–19, 130–31; Cost Plus World Market: 96tr; Courtesy of the Fine Arts Museums of San Francisco: 114tl; Courtesy of the Oakland Museum of California: 126tc, 126tr.

Enchanted Crystal: photo by David J Landry 104tl; Executive Suites: 149tl. Frey Norris Gallery: 42tl. Dave G Houser/Houserstock: 15cr, 18–19, 75tl. Ronald Martinez/ Getty Images: 73r; Terrence McCarthy: 56b; MGM/Ronald Grant Archive: 53tr; *Michael Jackson and Bubbles, 1988* by Jeff Koons/ Collection of the San Francisco Museum of Modern Art; Sean Moriarty: 74tr.

Paramount Pictures/Ronald Grant Archive: 16tr; Pink Club: Christian Horan Photography 71tl.

Redferns/David Redfern: 54tc; Rex Features 37cl, 53tl;

San Francisco Zoo/Jason Langer: 114c.

Robert Vente: 20b, 32c, 32b, 33t. 34tr. 35t, 61r, 72b, 74tl, 148tl, 149.

Warner Bros/Ronald Grant Archive: 53br; Jerry Yulsman: 52b.

For jacket credits see Contents page

All other images are © Dorling Kindersley. For further information see: www.dkimages.com.

Special Editions of DK Travel Guides

DK Travel Guides can be purchased in bulk quantities at discounted prices for use in promotions or as premiums. We are also able to offer special editions and personalized jackets, corporate imprints, and excerpts from all of our books, tailored specifically to meet your own needs.

To find out more, please contact:
(in the United States) **SpecialSales@dk.com**
(in the UK) **Sarah.Burgess@dk.com**
(in Canada) DK Special Sales at **general@tourmaline.ca**
(in Australia) **business.development @pearson.com.au**

Selected Street Index